100 ways to Photography

T h e   E x p e r t   a d v i c e

Choo Meng Foo has been a photographer since he was fifteen years old. At sixteen he had won overall best print (student section) for Asian Salon competition and his work had been exhibited in the National Museum, National University of Singapore and abroad. He went on to shoot for Tennis and Squash circles. Most recently his work had been featured in Asian Geographic Magazine, Silverlining, Wave, and One. His subject interest includes theatrical performance, portraiture, cityscape and arthropods. He has also given seminars and workshops on photography and digital post processing techniques.

100 ways to Photography

100 ways to Photography

The Expert advice

Choo Meng Foo

insecthunter.net
Singapore

For those who speak of photography and wrote with photographs.

Copyright (c) Choo Meng Foo, 2010
All rights reserved

The moral right of the author has been asserted

Printed in Singapore

Title: 100 tips of Photography
Author(s)/Editor(s): Choo Meng Foo
ISBN: 978-981-08-4375-5
Edition: New
Language: English Estimated date of publication: 2010-12-01 Format: Paperback / Softcover
No of pages: 100
Email: choomengfoo@gmail.com

Introduction 7
1. Fun 9
2. Know your camera 11
3. Depth of field (Dof) 13
4. Selecting shutter speed 15
5. Aperture 17
6. ISO 19
7. Shoot RAW 20
8. Pictorial differences in lenses 21
9. Hyperfocal point 22
10. Multiple exposures 23
11. Monopod 24
12. Bonding with your camera 25
13. Pirate light – feel, hear and see the lag 27
14. If you can't see it, you won't be able to shoot it 29
15. Focus and obliterate 31
16. Golden rule of third 33
17. Blue sky 34
18. Jump 35
19. Crystallising Water 36
20. Making faces 38
21. 100 shots within 10 minutes 39
22. Dusk 41
23. Night Scene 42
24. Tree Bark 43
25. Repetition 44
26. Coffee, food and wine 45
27. Reflection 46
28. Forest floor 47
29. Pose with strangers 48
30. Babies are spontaneous 49
31. Photographing in tight space 50
32. Mirror Mirror 51
33. Look for perspectives 52
34. The eye is the story 53
35. Emptiness 54
36. Simplicity, portraits on white 55

37. Festive Pattern 56
38. Portraiture and time of the day 57
39. Portraiture underwater 58
40. The lure of colour 59
41. Shooting in water using Point and Shoot Camera 60
42. Framing view 61
43. Shoot through foreground objects 62
44. Complementary 63
45. Do the opposite 65
46. Be mundane 66
47. Covered faces 67
48. Tilting the camera to create interest 68
49. Photographs attained meaning when they aged 69
50. Flaw makes a picture loveable 70
51. Creative Blur 71
52. The treasure is under your nose 72
53. Escape from the camera 73
54. Colour management 75
55. Blue tone 77
56. Sepia print 78
57. Pastelmatic 79
58. Posterization 80
59. The Beauty of Grain and noise 81
60. Crop away 82
61. Stitch up when the angle is not wide enough 83
62. Black and white HDR 84
63. HDR for Architecture 85
64. Imbue image with meaning 86
65. Know your uniqueness 88
66. Simplicity: One camera, one lens, one shot 89
67. Learning to ask 91
68. Shoot Portraits with Macro lens 93
69. Wide angle portraiture 94
70. Portrait lenses 95
71. Using 50mm 1.8 for portraiture 97
72. Shoot from high angle 98
73. Using Wide angle lens for event 99

74. Low angle shot 100
75. You are the zoom 101
76. Photograph those who want to be photographed 102
77. Train yourself to look into the eye 104
78. Have no fear 105
79. Selective focusing 106
80. The Sun is the heart 107
81. Shooting against the Sun 109
82. Shadow is light 110
83. Side lighting 112
84. Shooting landscape 113
85. Flowing energy 114
86. Master of time 115
87. Seize the right moment 116
88. Photography is discipline 117
89. Photography is joy 119
90. Not getting it is a feedback 120
91. Curiosity is not enough 121
92. A distilling process 123
93. Persistence 124
94. The descent 126
95. Sleight of space 128
96. Enter and leave yourself behind 130
97. I am the Servant 131
98. Dead and awaken 132
99. Keep a journal 134
100. Forgetting and contradiction 135

Acknowledgement 136

100 ways to Photography

Introduction

Photography is an art form.
The camera is the brush.
Light is the medium.
And you are the creativity.

Through 30 years of exploring photography, I realised that photography is not only about the camera, it is also about the photographer and the subject. My exploration oscillates between the camera and exteriority of the camera.

I learned all about the camera in the initial few years, my work was well received but I felt that I had hit a snag; I stagnated. I asked myself where do I go from here? Where is the limit of photography? Does my work need rejuvenation from outside of itself? Yes, after much searching and experimenting, I found various ways to raise my acuity, bringing my work to another realm. Here I would share some of these with you. Outside the camera, the horizon have expanded far and wide. I felt exhilarated and revitalised.

Take my inhibition, an instance of exteriority of the camera, by removing inhibition, portraiture takes on another pictorial landscape. Yes, by learning from psychology and neuro-linguistic programming, borrowing from their studies and practices, I learned to remove inhibition and my photographs take on new meaning.

This book will take you to greater height as a photographer. Follows the steps with discipline and more practices, you will definitely improve.

Some tips are easily grasped. Some have to be experienced before you understand them. Some needs faith to see the results. Some may seem a little odd. However, if you follow them, you would later discover their relevance. Then again, what works for others may not work for you, because we are all different. Try different ways of using these tips. There are no sequence in using this book, each tip is self serving, or it can be combined in various ways to suit your needs. Perhaps doing the opposite may serve you well too.

E-books, audio books and video books will be published in due time. So look me up on Facebook and join the 100tips Photography group. For those interested to get in touch with me, please email me at choomengfoo@gmail.com

1. Fun

We mustn't look at photography as a tedious, difficult and mystical art form, it is indeed fun and experimental. It is something we can do everyday to document our life and the world around us. When is the last time you had fun and you loved it very much? If you miss the fun, just do it again. Photography is similar. It is a process you enjoy and you want to repeat it.

Some great photographs are mere records of fun, experimentation or spur of the moment. The notion of fun enlightens the analytical mind. It opens up the intuitive and the subconscious mind allowing us to be free in our moments. We should not immediately reject the idea or feel uncomfortable whenever a new idea pops up in our mind. Take up the intuition and try it. Release your inhibitions. Free yourself from yourself. There is no other reason but you. Why not?

Just do it.

Of course sometimes you may need people to help you. Just ask. If you are rejected, you ask another person. Rejection should not generate shame or stop you from trying. You just need to try harder. It is a numbers game, if you ask ten people probably you will get one to agree to help, and if none agreed, then ask a hundred or thousand people, you are bound to find one that agree.

Many fun ideas came to me in the spur of the moment, such as jumping, the hundred shots in five minutes and the existing light macro photography. I feel the spontaneity, I hear the hearty laughter and I see the dynamic energy exploding in playful fun. Everything sparkles, feels lighter and easier to achieve. I take them as seriously fun and I create a body of work around a single idea. I learned from implementing the idea and read into the photographs. The reading process enriches and brings the fun to the finale. Eventually with enough work the idea can come to a form of fruition.

Fun needs time too.

When you are having fun, time flies and swoops by. Then you realise you need more time for fun. You make more time and live it to the fullest. Don't you want to live your life to the fullest? Of course you do. Then dive into it. Have FUN!

2. Know your camera

The simplest way to understand the camera is to see it from the perspective of light. Light illuminates all beings, whether they are material or ephemeral. You would ask why ephemeral? Light when going through air or vapour, show us its variations, take for example, in the morning when the sun rays filter through the moisture laden air, its paths are clearly seen, as the temperature rises, vapour disappears and the sun rays slowly disappear.

Light is the creator of the image. The camera captures the light and makes it permanent on digital sensor or film. Light has to be regulated and captured in the amount necessary to imprint an image on the sensor or film. How does the camera regulate the amount of light? Very specifically by 3 means: **shutter, aperture and sensitivity of the sensor.**

A Camera is built and designed with these three crucial mechanisms. The shutter determines the duration for the light to continuously flow onto the sensor and imprints on it. Light flows like water; it has volume, breath, width, density (intensity) and depth. The aperture, the iris, acts as a gatekeeper, it determines the size of the beam of light that would pass through and strikes the sensor. The sensor takes in only part of the light, depending on the size, usually rectangle in shape. The sensitivity of the sensor determines the volume of light that is required to make a visible image. The sensor' sensitivity can be raised or lowered.

Shutter speed is measured in 1, 1/2, 1/4, 1/15, 1/30, 1/60, 1/125, 1/250, 1/500, 1/1000, 1/2000, 1/4000, 1/8000 of a second. However, for simplicity, only the bottom number is shown on the camera, for 125 it means 1/125 of a second. So the bigger the number the faster the shutter closes, the less time the light has in striking the sensor.

The aperture closes and opens in different sizes. It resides in the lens. It is denoted by f-numbers, such as, f/1, f/1.4, f/2, f/2.8, f/4, f/5.6, f/8, f/11, f/16, f/22, f/32, f/45, f/64 and f/90. The aperture for most lenses would stop at f22 or f16. The smaller the f-number, the larger the aperture, which allows more light to pass through the lens.

The sensor's sensitivity is measured in ISO, 100, 200, 400, 800, 1600, 3200 and 6400. Better cameras can have higher levels of sensitivity than those I have listed.

Each of these sets of numbers is useful, because they can be arranged to compensate for one another. A single jump we can simply call a 'stop', so if the light meter tells us to use say, f16 at 1/125 of a second with ISO at 100, we can in effect use, f2.8 at 1/4000 of a second with the same ISO 100. We open up the aperture, count the stops, that is 5-stops, and then we compensate with faster shutter speed, add 5-stops to it and arrive at 1/4000 of a second. Simple! It works the same for ISO. Using the same example, I can have f2.8 at 1/8000 of a second with ISO 200. See the math? It is simple arithmetic.

Now we know how the camera functions. So go out there and experiment. Shoot at different shutter speeds, aperture sizes and ISO numbers. Notice how the images vary with different settings. There are real differences at different settings. Learn and notice the differences.

3. Depth of field (Dof)

How do we create depth on a 2 dimensional plane? Although photographs are captured from a three dimensional space, it is finally represented on a two dimensional plane. However, through some devises, we can create a stronger sense of three dimensionality. This three dimensionality is the connection to the story we are telling. Creating depth is one of the tools to tell a good story, especially a real one. One of the tools is using a combination of sharpness and blurriness to create a sense of depth. The subject in focus is sharp and clear, it becomes blurrier as it recedes away from us and it also becomes smaller naturally. Those that are nearer to us also get blurrier and they are larger. This way we emphasizes the subject matter and create a sense of depth. It is as if we can enter into the space of the photograph.

This clear and blur phenomenon is known as Depth of field (Dof). **This is achieved by varying the three components of the camera: the aperture, the focal length of the lens and the distance between the focus plane and the camera.** You would ask me the reasons for this phenomenon wouldn't you? Well, it is complex, and it takes much effort and time to understand, so tedious and intricate that I have to develop rules of thumb and fine-tuning them to achieve the result I want. Depth of field varies in degree since the three components have different settings.

We call a depth of field shallow when the acceptable clear and sharp area of the subject is less and a deep depth of field when a much larger area has acceptable clarity and sharpness. For a larger aperture, the depth of field becomes shallower. For example, when the focal length and the distance from the focus point is constant, an aperture of f2 will result in a shallower depth of field compared to using an aperture of f5.6. So try out your camera shooting from the same position and using the same lens, vary the aperture and make a series of photographs at a distance of about 1 metre from your subject. Get a feel of the resulting image and store the findings inside you, always apply it when photographing.

The longer the focal length of the lens, the shallower is the depth of field. For example, a lens with a focal length of 35mm would have a larger depth of field compared to a 200mm lens. Even at an aperture of say f3.5 for a 10mm lens focusing at more than 2 m away, everything in the picture will turn out sharp because it has a much larger depth of field.

The nearer the camera is to the focused subject, the shallower is the depth of field. So if you want to have a shallow depth of field, you move nearer to the subject. Even with a 10mm lens, you can create a shallower depth of field using this technique.

Try all the variations and see how they can compensate for one another, and notice the changes in the pictorial landscape of the photographs. Register those visual differences. Every compensation is different. They are subtly different. It is through the understanding of these differences and implementing them that you can create images that are uniquely yours.

4. Selecting shutter speed

Do you know what is shutter speed? It is the speed of the shutter curtain which opens and closes to allow light to fall onto the film or the digital sensor. Shutter speeds range from a few second to one-thousandth of a second. Some cameras have faster shutter speed of eight-thousandth of a second. Imagine splitting a second into 8000 slices. Wow!

The possibilities of using high shutter speed to freeze things in motion and see them as still as a rock is a miracle! So now you might think of shooting at eight-thousandth of a second and see some miracles. You shall be disappointed. You may think this tip is not working for you. Because many subjects can be frozen at a lower shutter speed, for example a general scenery, and you probably can go as low as one-thirtieth of a second, raising the shutter speed incrementally you wouldn't see any changes in the picture. I suspect our eyes see around this speed. It may be true that some people could see faster when they have special training or have a higher state of consciousness. For most of us, we can supplement 'the speed of our sight' through skilful use of the camera.

A rule of thumb is that if the subject looks stationary to you, chances are there would not be any difference when you shoot them at eight-thousandth of a second or one-sixtieth of a second. When a subject moves, you should use a shutter speed higher than one-sixtieth of a second.

The art of selecting shutter speed is based on a simple rule. Movement is relative, if you move at the same speed with your subject in the same direction there will be no movement in the image. If you move in the opposite direction at the same speed, the image moves doubly fast. You also realize as photographer, when hand holding the camera, we or the camera could move too! In fact, we are moving subtly and constantly, causing the camera to shake, commonly known as 'camera shake'. Long focal length lens magnifies camera shake. You need higher shutter speed for them. What constitutes movement is whether the image has moved at the film or sensor plane. If the image is displaced by one pixel, it is considered moved. When using a zoom lens, changing the focal length during exposure creates movement too.

As a rule, for the 35mm film camera to have clear pictures, the handheld shutter speed of the camera is inversely equivalent to the focal length of the lens. For example, a 50mm lens can be comfortably handheld at one-sixtieth of a sec or a 500mm lens can be handheld at five-hundredth of a second. For the non-full frame digital camera there is a factor to multiply for the focal length, say for the 3/4 format, the factor is 2. So a 50mm lens on the Lumix 3/4 format can be handheld at roughly one-hundredth of a second. With this simple rule, you can be sure of 'non-blur' pictures when you shoot. This is a simplified estimation, of course other factors play a part too, such as magnitude and direction of the movement, distance between the camera and the subject, and the steadiness of handholding camera.

You can also train yourself to shoot at a lower shutter speed by understanding posture and breathing techniques. Of course, the anti-shake cameras can be handheld at a slower speed.

Remember, **movement is relative**.

5. Aperture

There are a few factors that affect picture taking and one of them is aperture. Aperture is the iris of the camera and the size is denoted by the 'f' number. The smaller the f-number, the larger is the aperture. So a f1.0 aperture is larger than f16. The size of the aperture determines the amount of light falling on the light sensitive sensor. For a photographer, the fun of varying the aperture to control the look and feel of the image is important. Try shooting the same scene using different aperture settings and see if you notice the difference.

You may prefer one image to another because of its feel. Initially, I couldn't find a way to pin down this 'feel', after reading many photographic books and comparing many images. I learned to control this 'feel'. The common term to describe this 'feel' is 'Depth of field'. This term describes the sharpness of the image between the focused object and the distance before and away from it. As a simplified rule, small aperture such as f16 produces a deeper depth of field where most of the objects in the photograph will be sharp and with a large aperture such as f1.2 for a 50mm lens the shallow depth of field will render the focused object sharp and the rest of the objects not on the same plane, blur.

When the depth of field is well controlled, the image takes on clearer meaning. When to use different depth of fields (Dof)? For scenery, always use smaller apertures to ensure an end-to-end sharpness. For portraiture, use a larger aperture to bring the person into focus and the rest of the scene slightly blurry to reduce its significance. So get out there and start experimenting with aperture!

It is great fun to see the differences in the images made with different apertures. For those using a Point-and-Shoot camera, you can still see the difference by setting the preference for higher shutter speeds such as sport feature, inducing the camera to select larger aperture. The effect will be more pronounced, when you zoom in. Feel and see the difference. See if it works for you.

6. ISO

The 3 major components that have an impact on the exposure of photographs are: Aperture, Shutter Speed and film sensitivity or sensor sensitivity. Film sensitivity is measured by ISO, which is an abbreviation for International Standard Organisation. The numbers are in multiplication of 2. They range from 100, 200, 400, 800, 1600, 3200, 6400 to 12800, and so on. Each jump is considered as a stop and it is a corresponding stop with the shutter speed and the aperture. Why do they put two zeros behind the first digit? Probably this is to separate possible confusion with shutter speed numbers.

What is the impact on the picture when the ISO is set higher? For film, it becomes more 'grainy' as the ISO is higher, and it is determine by the type of film you use. For digital, the image becomes 'noisier'. Though this is a phenomenon of different ISO, but it has become the prejudice cultivated by many photographers. They considered grainy images to be 'low grade' photographs.

However, in the arena of the creative world, many people have fallen in love with grain. Grain appears in different sizes for film, unlike digital images that have discrete size for each pixel. Here we see subtle differences in the photographs taken by film and those taken by digital sensors. Film still has the lure which the digital camera cannot replace or duplicate. There are no 'better' or 'worse' medium of capturing the images, be it film or digital. I can still remember occasions when we deliberately use high ISO film such as Kodak Tri-X or the Ektacolor 1600 and push the film to higher ISO to create lovely grains that are mesmerising till these days. 'Pushing' is a process where we prolong the required timing for developing the film.

Remove the prejudice and see the 'noise' in another light which can make your photograph uniquely yours. Try it. I can already see the style and its use in fashion photography.

7. Shoot RAW

When I first bought my Digital Single Lens Reflex (dSLR), I shot in JPEG and RAW and scrutinised the pictures on the computer to see if there were visible differences between the two formats. After much scrutiny and checking with friends, we came to a conclusion. There is no difference between them. However I later realised the usefulness of RAW. On one occasion, I underexposed some pictures and because they were in RAW I could adjust them in the Canon Professional Application by raising the exposure by one stop. Some information is recovered in the shadow areas. Having room for recovery is an advantage of shooting in RAW.

Most RAW files are storing at 12 bits per colour and if we multiply the three different colours we get more than that of the JPEG, which is 8 bit per colour resulting in the possibility of only 16 million colours. Of course, most images will not contain so many colours at once. Another disadvantage of using JPEG is that it is a 'lossy compressed' file, which means some inherent information is removed during the compressing process. So it is better to store in RAW and retain all possible information.

Remember to shoot in RAW the next time.

8. Pictorial differences in lenses

I bet you had seen scene in the movie in which a huge truck was going to run over the hero, your heart beat in anxiety and you hoped fervently that he would get away safely. Of course he did. In fact, he was still a distance away from the speeding truck during the filming. The illusion of proximity between the machine and him is created using long focal length lens such as the 300mm.

There are differences in the picture rendition when lenses with different focal lengths are used. It is the perception of distance between the subjects in the scene. Our eyes have a focal length of around 40mm to 50mm which is perhaps one of the reasons why 35mm film cameras in the old days came with a 50mm standard lens. So we evaluate pictures according to our 'eye standard'. When we see images taken with a wide angle lens, we tend to see the space as huge and deep. However, if it is taken with a telephoto lens we see a compression of space between the subject and the background, we feel that they are nearer to each other.

Understanding the effect when using different lenses helps us to decide which lens to use when we are photographing to achieve our vision. Though we cannot recreate scenes with the flexibility of painting, we can understand the subtle differences that enhance the images we are snapping.

9. Hyperfocal point

Many years ago there were cameras known as fixed focus cameras. This cameras' lens had no focusing ring. There is no need to focus, you just point the camera and shoot. It is that simple. The images were acceptable for many people then, as long as they could see some semblance of the people they had taken. Perhaps there are still some in the market by obscure brands. However, people's expectations of a good photograph have risen and they prefer sharper and richer colour images.

We can replicate the same situation far better with more control using digital lens and camera. First, you set the lens to the Hyperfocal point. At this point, which is determined by the aperture we had set, within the distance between a point away from the camera to infinity, the image is acceptably sharp. This is known as the hyper-focal distance. Check the lighting condition and select the aperture and shutter speed of the scene, say if f8 is selected, check the colour of the aperture number f8, then refer to a set of vertical lines etched on the barrel of the lens. Say if f 8 is yellow, you then align the infinity sign to the right yellow line, now the camera is set to the high focal point. The left yellow line indicates the distance with acceptable sharpness immediately away from the camera. However, modern lenses have done away with the markings on the barrels. Don't be surprised if you cannot find it. Simply go to the Internet and look for pictures of old lenses which is of the same focal length and use it as an estimate for your newer lenses.

Once the camera is set, just point and shoot without setting the camera to autofocus or touch the focusing ring. The importance is seeing and shootings. Have no fear while shooting. Of course, the smaller the aperture, the deeper the depth of field, and the smaller the focal length the deeper the depth of field. For 10mm lens I believe at f16, you can shoot within less than half a metre to infinity with acceptable sharpness. So get out there, wave your camera at people and shoot your heart out!

10. Multiple exposures

There is a small catch on some film cameras to perform multiple exposures on the same negative. It is especially useful when we want to create 'twins' in the same photograph. We do a little handy work by slicing the lens cap into two equal halves; make two exposures on the same portion of the negative with first the left half of the lens cap removed and the second with the right side removed. Each time, the same person changes position on different exposures so that he can appear on both exposures. Now we have created a pair of twins on the same photograph.

I have not seen multiple exposures catch on Digital Single Lens Reflex (dSLR) or pocket cameras. It seems strange that this feature is removed. However, there are much more flexibility if you use a photograph manipulation application such as Photoshop or Corel Paintshop Photo Pro X3. Otherwise, for simple manipulation some free applications on the Internet can do too.

For creating multiple images of the same person on the same background, first mount the camera on a sturdy tripod, adjust the camera and frame a scene, visually decide where are the various positions the person is going to sit or stand. Ensure that the person do not overlap himself in the different exposures, otherwise the image will need serious masking, which may be considered tedious for many.

After shooting the four different images, bring them into Photoshop, now cut and paste the other three images onto the first image. Now use the marquee tool and draw over the person, complete the loop and do an inverse selection, then delete the selection. Continue to do the same for the others and soon you will have seen four similar persons in the photograph. Other applications can do this simple task too. Try it and have fun amusing your friends and family.

11. Monopod

I have been shooting photographs since I was fifteen years old and after thirty years I have not grown tired of it. I have grown to love seeing others in the viewfinder and I was not particularly bothered about not being in the picture. When I was courting, I brought tripod along to photograph my girlfriend and I together. It was clumsy, she was impatient and I could not capture the sweet moment. Emotions were stifled in front of the camera, and I did not take many photographs of us together.

One day, when I was forty, as I looked into the mirror, I realised my faced had changed so much. It looked interesting with long white hair and wrinkles. When I was much younger, I used to hunt and snap pictures of old people with interesting wrinkles. At that moment, I thought I was as photogenic as them. They were especially gorgeous when they were bathed by the early morning light. I saw a part of me was gone and I had not recorded much of it.

This starts me thinking about not leaving myself out of the picture when I am with friends and family members. I want to be included in the photographs. My solution was to use an extendable monopod that is light and handy. The monopod should have a ball head that can pan horizontally and vertically. With the monopod it is a snap to get the angle I want. Since then I have been including myself in many photographs whenever I travel with friends and family. The album is complete now. We love an unmanned camera and there are much more creative angles and viewpoints with the extendable monopod.

Get a monopod and start to include yourself in the picture. You will love it. Your family and friends will too!

12. Bonding with your camera

Treat your camera as your first love. If you do not love your camera, do not treat her with respect, care and patient, she will fail in time when you require her service. The camera is to the photographer, as the sword is to the swordsman or the rifle is to the sniper. They have to be treated with utmost respect. The bond you have with her is unbreakable.

Treat your camera like your lover!

When you bring her out, check that she is sparkling clean, no dirt or oil on the lenses, battery fully charged, memory card has enough space, the bag or pouch is in good condition to hold her, her strap is looking good and she is functioning. Do some test runs and shoot a couple of shots. When everything is fine, you are ready to go. For those who are going for a long journey, you need to bring spare batteries, a charger, an electrical converter, spare memory cards, cleaning pen and cleaning cloth. A raincoat for her to use during a shower would be sweet.

Spend some time memorizing all the functions and dials that put her into the state you prefer. Better still if your eyes are closed and you can still move the dials to the positions you want, especially those commonly used and frequently adjusted functions, such as Aperture Priority, Manual exposure, exposure compensation dial, ISO setting, playback, bracketing, etc. When you are shooting, handle her gently. If you are rough, she may get knocks and the worst is a bad fall. The secure way is to wind the strap around your hand or hang the strap over your neck to avoid dropping the camera accidentally.

When you return after the shoot, wipe her with a clean and try cloth, check that the lens is clean, the lens cap is snapped on, remove dust and place her in a dry cabinet or windy area. This will keep her away from fungus growth, which is a deadly sin and will cause irreversible damage. Importantly, develop the sensitivity of handling the camera, enjoy her performance and treasure her creation.

13. Pirate light – feel, hear and see the lag

All photographers are pirates of light; we steal the moment we treasure. To steal the precise moment we need to practise stealing. The camera shoots in an instant. Some can go as fast as 1/8000 of a second, and most is at least 1/1000 of a second. It is fast, but do we have a sense of this 1/8000 of a second? It seems implausible. Perhaps something less would seem plausible for us.

Imagine, the whole process of shooting, you see, feel and decide to depress the shutter. When your brain has decided, it sends an instruction to your finger to depress the shutter. The shutter release is a double action, first it instructs the lens to focus and the lens focuses then the button travels a very small distance further downward to trigger the electronic pulses to instruct the aperture to close the iris, the shutter opens and light falls on the light sensor. The sensor records the changes in electrical potentials. They are interpreted into RGB colours in 3 different layers, written in the memory buffer and then quickly transfer into permanent memory in the memory cards. We have pirated the image! Then we realise the image is slightly different from the one we have seen. Revisit the whole process and we realise, time and expression have changed as we depress the shutter. We call this a lag, a lagging behind of the actual image. Now, you realize you have stolen the wrong image. You despair, wondering how you can perfect the timing.

Here is a practice. Do this in a quiet place, until you are sensitive to your camera. Bring your camera to your eye, see the subject you are aiming, close your eyes, breath in, feel your breath, depress the shutter slowly, hear and feel the lens moving, then a beep sound, then the shutter snaps. Repeat the step until you can feel the entire lag. Now you should better the timing of your shots. If you still feel that you are not getting it, keep on practising until you are good at it.

Remember, you are a pirate that steals the moment you never see.

You see your treasure only when you have stolen it. You only have a feeling of the consciousness of what it is when you are stealing. Perfect your timing Pirate of Light!

14. If you can't see it, you won't be able to shoot it

If you are not aware of the surrounding when you are photographing, you wouldn't be able to see what is happening and be prepared to capture those precious moments. You have to learn to postulate how an event is going to unfold, and anticipate the location that would best capture the moment. You have to move quickly into position, aim and release the shutter, eternalising the split thousandth of a second into an image.

Raising your sensitivity, you will gain a heightened level of awareness.

We have five senses. Mostly, we only use our sense of sight and hearing to gain understanding of our environment. Practise this in the garden with eye closed, listen to all the sounds, smell the environment, discerning and separating differences in them, feel the brushes of breeze, smell the moisture and the temperature in it and taste the air. With more practices, our senses will improve. For sight, sit in corners of cafes, watch people's behaviour, see the light falling on surfaces, sense the colour changes as the day passes by, while tasting the coffee, hearing conversations, and smelling the different perfume.

Before getting into action, it is important to do a quick survey of the environment, decide on the course of action, conceptualise the imagery that would best describe your vision and inspiration. Give yourself at least 5-10 minutes to observe people and their activities before deciding what is worth shooting, from which location to shoot, the preferred composition and camera exposure setting. Seeing is the most important aspect of a good image, so practise seeing. It is a spiritual affair at its highest level of awareness, shooting it is a technical execution, a physical affair.

To capture a great moment, is the union of a spiritual and physical act.

15. Focus and obliterate

Unless we don't want to succeed, we need to learn how to focus and concentrate. Focus is a form of discipline, which is not unique to photography alone. Martial arts practitioners demand intense concentration and focusing power of themselves.

Yes, focusing is a form of power.

In photography too, we demand the same, we focus on the subject we are shooting. We are forced to focus when we lift up the camera and place it near our eyes. The viewfinder frames the view. We focus on the subject and when we are ready, we snap the picture.

I can still remember the thrill and excitement I had when I saw printed photographs. It was like magic. It is unlike today, you can review the image as you photograph. There was an anxiety period when we were shooting film. We shot and we could only get the photographs after 24 hours. It was considered speed processing, otherwise it would normally take 3 days to a week. Each shot was so precious as a roll of film consists of only 36 shots. We focused intensely and we did more. We learned the art of obliterating.

Obliterating is the art of removing the unwanted bits and pieces of an image that happens to be included with the subject we are framing. They distract the viewer from the subject or the meaning we are trying to portray. Obliterating is done when we look into the view finder, we focus on the subject, check the background, deciding how to simplify the background by moving left, right, up, down and adjusting the aperture to control depth of field. We obliterate to make the background recedes into a supporting role, thereby emphasising the subject.

Obliterating is also taking a step back from the focused subject without loosing sight of it and making adjustments to further enhance the subject through manipulating the background.

Inadvertently, we forgot that the main subject only stood out because it was situated in the appropriate background. It is like a star needs her fans or stars need darkness to shine. Obliterating the light from the sun we see the stars in the distance. Light needs shadow to reveal itself.

So learn the art of obliterating and make yourself shine like a star!

16. Golden rule of third

Rules are rules. If we cannot remember how they came about or the reasons for them, it is unacceptable and we are labelled as one of the 'blind followers'. We are indeed ignorant, irrational, superstitious, unreasonable, confused, not analytical, and eventually labelled as not good at what we are doing? But seriously, if something works and works beautifully, do we really need reasons for them. Rules become our habit and they are a part of us. Do we need a reason for everything? Some would say 'yes' and bring it to the extreme with an affirmative – yes, yes, and yes. They are the righteous, serious people. For others like me, I grow older and become forgetful, more experienced too. Because I remembered the rules and focus on getting it right, not the reasons, and I got better photographs. Knowing the reasons is not good enough to snap a good picture, as knowing how well each lens and camera performs, does not necessarily make you a good photographer. Experimenting or using the rules to your advantage does.

Here is a great rule: **The golden rule of third.** Divide the picture into 3 parts, vertically and horizontally. You should have 9 squares. There are 4 intersecting points, the point where the 2 vertical and horizontal lines intersect. These 4 points are where we place the focus of the picture. This rule works most of the time. It has become my habit and characterised most of my shot.

Try this rule. If you don't like it, discard it and create your own compositional rules.

Glorify your rules and make them work for you.

17. Blue sky

I loved photographs with blue skies when, starting at fifteen, I was given my first camera. They always made me happy. Somehow my sky in my photographs did not turn out so blue then. I began to take interest in spotting blue sky. I will grab my camera and start shooting whenever I spotted them. Watching the sky became an obsession.

After so much watching and shooting, I finally understood how to get a nice deep blue sky. Having blue sky is important.

One cannot fake a blue sky, no matter how good he is with photograph retouching software.

The blue hue is reflected in every bit of other material, which is why changing the sky blue with retouching application, isn't going to cut it. To get deep blue sky, spot a blue sky day, choose lightly coloured subjects, underexpose 1/2 to 1 stop for the sky. Viola! You've got deeper blue. And it is dramatic too in Black and White!

With this technique, I always get lovely deep blue.

18. Jump

If you have ever had difficulty coming up with interesting poses for your friends or subjects, I suggest you ask them to jump or leap up into the air when posing. It is fun and thrilling. I have done many jumps myself and snap others jumping as well. I realized one great phenomenon; it is really difficult not to be yourself in mid air, in that instance, your struggle, unease, fear, apprehension, or triumph shows. The shutter speed should not be less than five-hundredth of a second. Any slower, the jump cannot be frozen and it will result in blurry photographs.

Shoot from low angle. The jumpers would appear to achieve greater height. Use a wide angle lens to further accentuate the height, their legs, and you've gotten a dynamite leap-up.

People jump with all kinds of styles and moves. The excitement is notched up when leaping in public with outlandish, historical landmarks as the backdrop. Looking from posterity, you would see the value of this seemingly frivolous act.

Try it and have fun. I have derived a lot of fun out of it and continue to do so.

19. Crystallising Water

On many occasions, I watched and photographed from the sideline of the pool while my children were having fun splashing water at each other. Water fight is their favourite activity. When their hands sweep, water will fly and morph into multiple forms and shapes. Water is malleable. It flows and searches for the lowest point before it settles. It can pound and crash to penetrate rocks and stones. Water is a symbol of strength, an affable strength, though seemingly weak, could penetrate the hardest of elements.

Bruce Lee once described the secret to martial art – 'flows like water'.

Water has an intriguing personality. Water turns into ice, becomes really hard, shave and chisel them, and it forms captivating ice sculpture. Shoot it with high shutter speed when it swirls and fly through the air, bathed it in warm greasy sunlight and achieve those wildly fabrications, unimaginable till it is frozen.

Before releasing the shutter, anticipate, best guess, the resulting image. The actual image captured is known only when it is reviewed. The lag between what we saw and captured, makes snapping flying water all the more interesting and fascinating.

Every image involving water is different, unexpected and mesmerising.

Choose a bright and sunny day with deep blue sky for the shoot. Use a lens with focal length of at least 100mm. Set the aperture to the largest, say f2.8. The shutter speed should not be less than one-thousandth of a second and the background should be dimmer than the foreground. You can get better results by getting down to the level of the water, so lie prone down if you need to. There is nothing awkward adopting this position. Shoot wildly and capture those crystallised water! At the speed of above four thousand of a second, the water becomes a morphed transparent mass that reflects the environment. It is coincidental art!

Who is the artist? The kids, the water or you, the photographer. But one thing we cannot deny, we have fun.

20. Making faces

Hate them or love them, make faces at them. Make faces at babies to entice them, to smile and giggle. Stick out your tongue and pull down your lower eyes lids to scare someone. Stick your fingers into your mouth and drag it wide open and squeeze your eyes as narrow as you can go; you'll look ridiculously funny. Funny, distorted faces, they all make memorable images and memories. You would enjoy young children doing the same. They will look cuter, making faces than you do. Wouldn't you love to have an album full of faces, though funny but exuding joy and life? Who wouldn't?

Faces, especially when they are funny and joyful, look wonderful.

Invite your friends, family members and children to make some faces. When they oblige, you will have a memorable time. Start snapping them. They will look even more charming in posterity.

21. 100 shots within 10 minutes

I have been shooting portraits with existing light for many years and I have been thinking, what is the best way to bring out someone's personality? Previously, I shoot them when they went about doing their usual stuff. Initially they would feel uncomfortable. They would react to the presence of the camera and become self-conscious. Only by staying around with them for some time, then I could capture them in their nature. However, the images have the effect that they were being watched. These images are weak in connecting with the viewers. Their eyes did not make that connection.

The photographer has to learn how to communicate with his subject and capture the instance when the subject is being herself or himself. Photographers need practices to perfect their skill. Here is a practice I have created and tried myself. The practice lasts only 10 minutes, after which there should not be any more shooting. This is important to put the subject and you into this frame of mind of only 10 minutes, you or the subject are going to hurry through the process such that your subject has little time to ponder and try to put up a front of herself. Never give any idea to the subject how to pose or how she or he should stand. Ask him or her to be natural. What ever comes to hers or his mind, they would immediately enact it. You, as the photographer, should react to the subject with immediacy, moving in and out, up or down, left or right, with the camera. The practice is solely based on the fact that the duration is short and 100 shots are fired, with little time to think and act, thereby in this speedy reaction and action forced both the subject and photographer into being their true selves, revealing the true personality of the subject through the eyes of the photographer. As the photographer, remember to focus on the eye of the subject, as the eye is the window into the heart.

I made some observations and learned from this practice. First I realised that sometimes, when the lens was still focusing I snapped, resulting in blurred images. Some subjects never paused for the camera to focus and snap. Exposure had to be adjusted constantly as I moved and shifted my position while the model reacted with shifting and relocating her position. Exposure had to be adjusted constantly when I had shifted while the lighting varied constantly. I realised that I had to improve my way of switching the camera's dials without lifting my eye away from the subject.

Practise, and more practices are required to perfect my skill in handling the camera.

To reiterate, I have to wait for the camera to focus, and upon focusing, compose, when the subject's mood is right, depress the shutter release.

There are multiple considerations, including exposure. I have to develop a way of capturing those signature moments. It is a great practice to do. Try it!

22. Dusk

There is a certain rhythm and colour shift when the sun glides from the East to the West.

It is quite an experience when we feel the sun rays early in the morning, watching the sun rising slowly and hearing the animals making their morning call. In dusk, we too could feel the tiredness in the atmosphere as the sun drags itself down the horizon, seeing the people returning to their homes, and hearing the returning calls of the birds before they rest for the day.

Dusk speaks a lot to us, makes us feel restful, and we see the accomplishment of our day's effort. The yellow tint of light in the setting sun washes all the material it comes into contact with, the wall, the road, the people and the sky. The sky becomes bluer, gradually fading into yellow as it gathers around the sun. Shadow become elongated when the rays fall on them. Dusk is a terrific scene. When photographing dusk, try photographing the yellow tint and the elongated shadow. They make magic and emphasize the materiality of the scene. Choose any architecture, facade, wall, door, entrance, or plaza. Look for dusk related activities. Compose, release and make permanent, dusk in action.

23. Night Scene

To see colourful glittering lights in the night is both romantic and fascinating. They are brighter and bigger than the twinkling star above the sky. Nights are filled with a sense of romanticism; darkness is mystical. Inducing our imagination to run wild. We become more creative, filling in when there are no lights.

With digital cameras, we could snap and immediately review the image, making it easier to shoot night scene, except that there may be difficulty in automatic focusing. However, the recent cameras throw a continuous ray of red light to ease focusing. Camera can be handheld easier when fitted with a wide angle lens; I can manage to shoot at an average shutter speed of 1/25 of a second with a 35mm lens.

With a tripod you can use slower shutter speed and car lights turned into streak of yellow or read line.

Try using less than 30 sec and see the car lights turn into frenzy display of colourful lines.

24. Tree Bark

I love to see the furrows, fissures, plates and texture on the tree trunks; they are nature's abstract art. I am always intrigue by them. Macro lenses are useful in recording them. They are stationary, unlike the leaves and branches that sway in the slightest breeze. They are symbols of sternness and rigidity, representing strength, perseverance and fulfilment.

Barks can come in many forms, some have deep furrows, some peel, some are colourful and some smell terrific. There are also unique marks made by animals; some hide in the bark's minute crevices. The most common dwellers are the beetles, the scorpions, the spiders and bugs. Together they form an interesting composition on the abstract terrain. Side lighting is preferred, rather than direct illumination. Move around the trunk, study and select the interesting portion before snapping them. Take your time, bark don't runaway.

25. Repetition

There are many recurrence and repetition in life. However, when we observe them carefully, we find some slight variations in each of them. Such is the uniqueness of nature. In things manufactured by man they will be uniquely different only after deterioration or repeated used.

Repetition is fascinating; it allows us to see the grandiose of nature when it is repeated countless time. When we take in the breath and depth of it, we are totally mesmerised. Repetition makes good subjects, whether they are animate or inanimate things. The numbers, even as little as five similar copies, would somehow create the effect. We love to watch repetition but we are intolerant of recurring mistakes or recurring occurrence, like having the same breakfast everyday.

I love to look out for repetition especially when they are lined up in a continuous row. Try to take some repetitions and look out for their differences, comparing them is quite an enjoyment.

26. Coffee, food and wine

Have you ever run out of subject to take? I have not, in my 30 years of shooting pictures. Time changes the urban and natural landscape; equipment changes from film to digital; the magical darkroom reduces to the simplicity of a digital application; the camera becomes a necessity; photography becomes essentially a language. We are in an ever changing world in need of speedy, effective communicating skill.

You want to practise. Do you eat everyday? You do. So shoot what you eat. Food, coffee and wine make good practices! Spare fifteen minutes before each meal, shoot, relax your nerve then down the meal before going back to work. You don't need a special camera to shoot food. Point and Shoot, or the dSLR will suffice. One good thing is: they are still and you can arrange them as you wish. Making picture is easy too. Set the camera to macro, compose and fire away. This is definitely the easiest way to have fun and learn about photography.

Try! Shoot, eat and shoot the left over. Do something different before each meal.

27. Reflection

Reflection distorts images. Be creative with reflection and reality would take another form. During Christmas, the metallic balls hanging from Christmas tree produce warp, surprising images. Shoot into the balls. If it's not Christmas, look for reflection off building facades or glass surfaces. Move in close, compose, watch the image changes on the reflective surfaces, seize the right moment and zap it.

Water is also a good reflective medium too. The lotus ponds, swimming pools, lakes and reservoirs amplified the subjects. **Be inventive, be experimental, be bold.** Look for reflection and create.

28. Forest floor

Nature walk, a stress releasing activity, we all have done it. Morning walks are usually filled with cool fresh air, we hear the birds chirping, and some insects stridulating somewhere among the foliage. We always look up or straight ahead, seldom do we pay attention to the forest floor that we are treading, except, when there are fallen trees, steep slopes or potholes.

We look outside and take for granted those that are near us, lest those beneath us. We look forward and seldom at what we already have. We demand more and have new desires once the old ones are fulfilled.

Perhaps we should take a pause and look right underneath our feet when we take nature walk. I discovered its beauty when I took a closer look, I paused, bent down, inspected and scrutinised it. I found its texture and colours immensely beautiful. With a camera of only a million pixels set to macro, I started to shoot them, made multiple images, and overlapped the shots such that I could stitch then using software.

I was wowed over when they were stitched together. The application I used came with the camera and it is a nice way to expand my repertoire to include a variety of subject matters.

29. Pose with strangers

We love to pose with great scenery or places of interest, and we do not like to include stranger in the photographs. Sometimes we have to wait until the scene is cleared of stranger before we snap our own. Some years back, a friend persuaded me to pose for him in a busy street, strangers never stop flowing beside me, he insisted to shoot and I gave in. To my surprise, I loved the photograph. It was a revelation! When we disregard the mess of people around us, we begin to get a better expression of our subject, the incidental inclusion of others, in fact, provide vital information to the image, contrast or compliment the image. It adds interest and allows a certain chance encounter which surprises, seduces and validates.

Now, I always look for opportunity to include people and incorporate them into the photographs. Timing it, such that I will only snap when they move into perfect composition. They also provide a sense of spontaneity for my picture. Co-opting stranger into the photographs help to resist the norm. Once this psychological hurdle is trounced, your photographs attain more meaning.

30. Babies are spontaneous

I remember when I had my first new born, I was overwhelmed with joy and anxiety. There were many things to learn and overcome.

One thing which I was grateful till today was to document their facial expression, and details of their hands, fingers, ears, feet and toes.

They looked so perfect and exuded a certain translucency which illuminated through the skin. I was mesmerised.

I used one of the earliest digital Canon cameras of only 350 thousand pixels. It was adequate for taking close-up of baby. Of course, it was a shame compared to today's lowest end of the Point and Shoot (PNS) cameras, but I had no regret for I had those images. He has grown to be a teenager. I wouldn't have those images if I waited until now for the perfect camera.

With today's dSLR, you can achieve better result. For a simple, no frill set-up, use a 50mm lens, the cheapest standard lens made by most manufacturers. Shoot with maximum aperture, it creates shallow depth of field putting the background into bokeh and the subject in focus. Arranged the baby on a white bed sheet near the balcony, where the light is diffused and soft. It models the baby well. Keep shooting as baby moves continuously, every picture is different, and baby is a joy to watch. They are expressive and cute. The photographs look more charming when in Black and White.

If you have babies, you should start snapping them with macro lens. Otherwise, ask someone to allow you to snap photographs of their babies and feel the joy of life evolving.

31. Photographing in tight space

Old age is fearful for many of us. Ageing elegantly have been intriguing me for some time. After the age of thirty-four, I could feel my fitness deteriorating and I have to keep up with regular exercise to maintain my fitness and energy level. The fear has kept me going until now, and I must say it works. Perhaps I take after my mum, she is still working and happy at seventy.

When asked how did you grow so old, Teresa Hsu, our most admired centenarian, at the age of 112, punned that she forgot to die. We had to laugh. Her alertness and pun stirred the deepest ocean of our consciousness. She was a guest at our class. It is during such occasion that we wouldn't want to miss recording them.

Fortunately, I had a 10-22mm wide angle lens which is necessary when shooting in tight spaces such as small classroom with many people. Although there are distortions at both sides of the photograph, where people seem larger and fatter, everyone is clearly visible in the photographs.

I call this dumb shooting, because the wideness of the lens causes such deep depth of field, no focusing is needed, just point and shoot. My favourite act is to stick it at rooms' corner and shoot blind. This is especially useful shooting toilets' interiors. This lens has served me well for architectural and interior shots.

32. Mirror Mirror

I must say, I am glad that I wear camera everywhere I go, a habit which I have acquired when I was working as city planner. I use it to photograph document, sites, reports and bill boards. It's both my journal and information gathering tool. Thanks to the manufacturer, today's digital point and shoot cameras are small and light weighted, a gem to carry around.

The added benefit I discovered is photographing my children. Opportunity arose while we were shopping for new clothes during one of the Christmas – the mirrors along the changing room. The multiple mirrors positioned outside and inside the changing room became a perfect place to creatively multiply images. We posed, realigned the mirrors and doors, shifted position, experimented and did many shots. It was great bonding with my kid. We were playful.

Time was well spent shopping and interacting with the children. Photographing my children kept them active and occupied, otherwise they would have gotten bored easily. Did you have the same experience when shopping with young children? I believe you would have. Try playing with the mirrors when you next visit the changing room, you can snap yourself too. Grown up make good subject too.

33. Look for perspectives

It is a challenge to create a feeling of three-dimension space on a two-dimensional plane. One ways is using diminishing lines. Brunelleschi and Leonardo da Vinci were the first few painters that had used the technique of perspective to create drama and realism in their paintings. The interior of corridors and alleys provide the diminishing lines to create one-point perspective.

Perspective adds a sense of scale, proportion and realism to the photographs.

When photographing interiors and streetscape, try looking for them, it brings more focus to the subject matter.

34. The eye is the story

When I am touched by portraits, I always wonder, how did that connection happened and what was it in the portrait which triggered it. It dawned on me one day. It is the eyes that spoke and made that connection.

As the cliché goes, **the eye is the window into the soul.**

So, for a good portrait, the eyes are the window into your subject which communicates a story, a feeling, an emotion or plight. In Mona Lisa, her eyes and the smile feature prominently, engaging the audience, creating a psychological dialogue. Therefore, to engage the audience, the eyes of the subject must engage the camera's lens, through which the audience see the picture, through which the audience make the connection, through which the picture wrote the text that words cannot describe; they touch.

Getting the eyes to speak through the camera is a practice which can be perfected. Wouldn't you want to perfect your skill at taking good portrait? Yes, you want to do that and you should make it a point to continue doing it. It's a simple and repetitive, nothing so complex, just practise, practise and more practices. By the time you had shot 10,000 portraits, you would have learned and experienced the way to create portraits that engage the soul.

This is one rule that I have never disregard – focus at the eye nearest to you when snapping.

It has remained till these days. Some rules are meant to be broken, but this is one classic rule which is hard to be broken. Stick to it and I believe some good portraits will come out from you.

35. Emptiness

Looking at some of the works by fellow photographers, we could be inspired and fired up. We see another perspective through their eyes mediated by the photographs. They are not necessary shots taken with great cameras or lenses, Leica or Hasselblad. Importantly they communicate and touch us deeply. One such recurring theme is emptiness.

Emptiness always returns to us whenever we are in a state of bewilderment.

It inspires me to return to words that I had written while searching for the meaning of life. Now, how do we use the language of photography to speak out this inherent emptiness that is always there waiting to return to you and me. It is the great emptiness of life and being. Without emptying, how can we make space to be filled? Here is my attempt to speak to you about emptiness.

Here is an intentional search for the imagery to portray a certain state of mind that I have so that I can communicate that state to you. In contrast, most other photographs are coincidence and discovery. I discovered and documented them when I am roaming the street. I scrutinised the subject to bring out something that is already there or within the subject. Whereas, this is a different attempt. It is to compose the imagery that speaks on my behalf, about emptiness.

If you feel empty, use your camera and speak out. Don't fake it.

We could see it through your vice. Be honest, be expressive, most of all be your self when you speak.

36. Simplicity, portraits on white

Things were simpler when we were younger. As we passed adolescence, things get a little more complex, and we began to have more responsibilities. The books we studied become thicker as we graduated from primary school to secondary school, then college and eventually university. Some books we used, weigh closer to a kilogram. However, as we grew older, we yearn for simpler things. **A reversal of sort, from a hectic urban life we seek a simpler and more peaceful existence.**

In portrait photography too, we turned to an all white background so that we can rid all distraction and focus on the subject, the person. We seek simple and natural lines that tell the true story of the subject. We prefer light colour clothes which is subdue. We demand that the subject be herself or himself. No elaborate pose or staged posture. In short no deliberate arrangement, no heavy make up, no strong colours. We request the subject to move, give a smile, turn around, face the camera and smile again. Some rapid firing and all those natural action will be recorded. Voila, it is done! Here, stand before us is the natural portrait.

Try it. You may not be comfortable in the beginning, neither is your subject, but you will get use to the simple style and get better at it. After all, you loose nothing by trying. Nothing, except those complexities of equipment and accessories.

37. Festive Pattern

During festive seasons, such as Christmas or Chinese New Year, the amount of goodies that caught our attention was mind-boggling. Goodies laid out in patterns naturally attract us. Who could resist the buying frenzy in such festive mood? Our right brain becomes so fired up that we purchase them without hesitation.

One way to say no to temptation could be just recording the patterns and comforting ourselves that we had a piece of great memory and excitement.

It may be a good way to fulfil our desire. So bring along your camera when you go shopping this season. Shop and shoot away.

38. Portraiture and time of the day

Have you ever wonder why the portraits that you had taken in existing lights are always not as great as those you had seen in galleries? It is not because they had used filled-in lighting or they had expensive equipment. If I tell you that by waking up early you can improve, would you make the effort to wake up early? It is as simple as that. You would ask why it is so.

It is all about the angle and the intensity of the sun light.

When the sun is rising, the intensity is lower, it does not blind the eyes, the eyes is wide open, and they look more beautiful. They connect well with the viewers in warmer light. When the sun rises higher, the sun angle becomes more acute with the face, causing the eyes' sockets to be darker and our eyes have to squint to reduce the glaring light. All these have an adverse effect on the face. The face becomes less attractive.

I always prefer dawn to dusk, because it is cooler, quieter, and there is more moisture and ions in the air. The invisible moisture, in minute particles help to lighten the scene as it fade slowly into the distance. The morning air, fills with ions, make us feel energised and ready to go. Dusk's atmosphere is filled with dust from vehicles and factories, laden with repulsive and dry particles. Dusk, for those working from nine to five or later, is a sign of tiredness and dread. Although the sun angle probably has the same effect but our state of mind is different in the morning and evening. Of course, if I am watching the sun setting at a beach resort and I have been relaxing all day, it is a great moment to wrap up, and become the finale of the day. It is an exception.

You should try portraiture in the early morning and see the improvement you will be making.

39. Portraiture underwater

After more than thirty years photographing people and street scene, it would be fun shooting portraits underwater. One thing about portraiture is capturing the essences of the person and less about the technical excellence of the photographic equipment. Many of us are very relax and comfortable in the water. When we want to relax, we go to the beach or the pool for a swim. We clear our senses and thoughts by floating in weightlessness. If you have problem shooting your love ones or models, get them to the beach or even better, photograph them in water and underwater. They will be so relax and you as the photographer would feel the same too. All would be fun and the photographs would turn out great too.

The bubbles and effervescence, spewing from the mouth and around the body is such a miracle to watch and experience.

Having one's portrait taken underwater is a rarity.

Make them feel like celebrities and you would be a great photographer. Seriously, how many of us get a chance to have our photographs taken under the water? Few can say yes I had been taken underwater. They are the fortunate few.

40. The lure of colour

Would you like to attract more viewers to your images? I would. I realized one of the predominant factors is colour. Use more saturated colours and your viewership will rise. Colour has unlimited power to attract. It accentuates emotion. The effect is so compulsive that some photographers would increase the saturation of the photographs taken to give it an extra punch. Although some would want the colour to be as accurate as the actual scene or the subjects, for the majority of us it is not the case. 'Sunflowers', by Vincent Van Gogh is so captivating because of the saturated colours. He applied paint directly from the tube onto canvasses. The feeling and emotion expressed is more real to the audience than the exact colour of the scene.

We prefer to experience the emotion convey by the photographs then without the emotion. We want to feel life and its vitality.

Look for colourful subjects and scene. Try it and see what great result you can achieve, and share with your friends some of your successes. You will discover that they are attracted to colourful images.

41. Shooting in water using Point and Shoot Camera

Did you ever want to snap images of your children having fun in the swimming pools or water theme park? Of course all of us as parents love to have memories of our children when they were young. We want to capture these happy moments permanently before they grow up and have their own lives. I used to stay away from the water and used the long telephoto lens to capture them. I was not participating in their fun. I prefer to be part of the fun, wouldn't you? I was glad when Olympus launched their tough Camera series which is shock proof, weather proof and waterproof. Most of all I found it simple to use.

I took my Olympus (Oly for some people) for a dip with the kids in the pool. The day was rather cloudy and the tiling of the pool was not so colourful. Eventually I decided to give the photographs a monochromatic effect. **The importance of the images is the memories of good time** and monochromatic effect emphasizes the emotional impact, wouldn't you agree?

I notice these images, in the midst of their action, defied the notion of gravity. They were slanted, creating more dynamism and allowing immense flexibility in composition. I love to see the water freezes in mid air, it is like crystal, bright sunlight is necessary for using high shutter speed. For cloudy day, due to the slow shutter speed, splashes become a white shade of morphic forms. If it is a cloudy day, try again another day with abundance daylight and a high shutter speed. I would suggest you go out there, grab or borrow a waterproof camera, experiment and share the photographs with friends and family members. It will be a great joy.

42. Framing view

Have you noticed work of art comes with framing? Some frames are so elaborate that they have gold trimming? Modern electronic such as television and digital display also adopted framing design. Of course, it becomes the ultramodern look when the frame is removed.

Framing is a terrific way to dress up the image with a decorative border.

It makes the viewer concentrate on the subject. Using door frame or object to frame, draws our attention towards the subject.

I find this particularly useful when I was shooting in Chinese Garden because part of the garden design is to draw visitors' view towards nature with a variety of windows and entrances, creating series of interestingly framed views.

43. Shoot through foreground objects

Being curious animal, we love to peer into other's affair or watch others from a safe unobtrusive position. Did you ever peer out from the hotel room and watch the street or your neighbours from your discreet windows?

This method works well with a long focal length lens. Position the lens with foreground object such as plants or sculpture. Find gap or hole for the lens to peer through it. Use a big aperture to create a shallow depth of field with the focus on the subject.

With big aperture the foreground will be blurry. The foreground and background enhance the sense of depth for the photographs.

You will love this effect when photographing people or your love one. It has a very romantic feel.

44. Complementary

What is knowledge or knowing? How did thought become and the mind grasp the knowledge of it? This has been my search for a long time. I learned from the oldest text written by Lao Zi, a Chinese philosopher who lived around 500 B.C., his life and date of birth is still a mystery and debated till these days, known as the Dao De Jing. In it, he pointed to the complementarism of the opposite as our path to knowing. It is through these differences in opposite polarities that we make conscious references to things and their characteristics. When we say something is beautiful, in our mind, we have something that serves as a reference as being ugly. If we do not have the reference, the concept of beauty becomes inconceivable, an unknown, which would not exist in our consciousness.

So benevolent comes with malevolent, good with evil, things with nothing, simplicity with complexity, long with short, leading with following and music with noise.

Photographs provoke emotion and thought through visual means. It is a form of visual text. It is a direct record of reality and its clarity is made obvious by the same thought process of complementary elements in the photographs.

Light can only have impact when it is contrasted with darkness.

The intensity of colours can only be loud and saturated when it is backed by no colour as in white and black. So a complex subject should be enhanced by a plain background. Focus is made sharper and emphasized with a bokeh backdrop. Understanding the effect of complementary elements is one of the ways to speak and portray successfully the photographic message.

Complementary is a wonderful tool for encoding messages. It speaks with both polarities to our consciousness and verbalises the visual text inherent in the images we have captured. Run through the image in your mind, in a quick and intuitive manner, incorporate complementary elements and your photography will take on immense clarity. This improves your message wouldn't it? You will benefit from this realisation. Compare your previous images and those that you have purposefully incorporated complementary elements. Notice the clarity you have achieved.

45. Do the opposite

To be good in photography is not just about concentrating on photographic technique alone. Photography is an art which requires simultaneous development of the individual, for example the love for painting, music, philosophy, architecture, culture, physics, geography, mental strength, physical prowess, social behaviour, etc. I would recommend any photographer to read voraciously, because inspiration and parallel can be drawn from them. Sigmund Freud's idea of the unconscious mind have been inspiring a generation of people in different fields: in art, the Dadaist movement, Dali as the most celebrated; in writing, the technique of automatic writing, W. B. Yeats in 'A Vision'; in psychoanalysis, it is the central theme of study; in language, Lacan's linguistic unconsciousness.

We learn from outside of photography to circumscribe a larger landscape in the exploration of photography.

My thought took a skip after reading Paul Arden's 'Whatever You Think, Think the Opposite', I was inspired to take some dead insects instead of those alive and kicking. 'Photograph dead roses instead of the live roses which thousand of photographers had been photographing' kept ringing in my ears. So I spotted the most common of all dead insect – a dead ant hanging by a silk thread swinging in the breeze.

While I was photographing, I was constantly pondering how did he died? Am I able to investigate the death of an ant? Very interesting indeed! It could make a good detective novel, unravelling the live of the micro-world. Am I autistic, like Mark Haddon had written? Who cares! I want to be a kid again, pursuing the trivial.

46. Be mundane

Sometimes life is so mundane that you cannot figure out interesting things to photograph. Once I stayed in my uncle's pig farm. The stench was so strong that I couldn't think of anything else to avoid except his pigs. I had gone around his house but found nothing that interests me. Eventually, challenged by the pungent smell. I took up the courage to do the most mundane – snapped photographs of his pigs and piglets.

Life does not always smell of roses or jasmine, sometimes the most mundane could turn out to be something good.

Once awhile doing the 'abnormal' challenges our tolerance and adaptability.

Some years later I took a second look at the photographs and felt sad about their lives. I put together a PowerPoint slide show for their plight.

Don't be despaired when you find life mundane. Record your feeling and state of mind. It could be meaningful when you reflect on them later.

47. Covered faces

Often when I roam the street to practise photography, after compositing the image, I would wait for pedestrian to complete the scene. Sometimes the pedestrian would walk right next to the camera and than covered her face. I thought she has ruined and wasted one of my shot, and felt mis-opportunity over it. This had occurred so often. I began to ask myself, did it really ruin the image or it had added a sense of reality to the scene, reflecting a certain culture and social norm of the place. My conclusion was eventually to accept their behaviour and consider the photographs as well taken, whether with covered face or face.

I learned to accept the nature of human behaviour and record them nevertheless.

Slowly we would ignore the face and see more meaning from their action and dressing. Often we value more of the human face and devalued the rest of our being. Often we are so affected by good looks that we forgot the beauty exuding from the rest of our body. In fact, we pay more to groom the face than the body; such is our bias towards the body.

Now I would go on and shoot covered up faces. Won't you do the same after considering the prejudice we have? Persuade yourself to try something different and see how you feel about it.

48. Tilting the camera to create interest

You would have noticed the diminishing perspective lines when you point your camera upwards or downwards. You felt the dynamism. You spent considerable more effort in getting the view horizontal.

Why not let the camera tilt?

Tilting the camera can create an entirely new perspective of a normal scene and give it interest. This is especially so when shooting architecture. The views get distorted with exaggerated perspective especially when wide angle lenses are used. Tilting emphasise the perspective and illustrate the intention much better.

49. Photographs attained meaning when they aged

Are you one of those who roamed the street with a camera in hand? Those were the days when we roamed the street with precious little Single Lens Reflexes documenting street life. We spent our time learning through observing and recording lives. Most street life had changed and it changes frequently. I had won many prizes and exhibited in a number of exhibitions, made it to radio interview and the mainstream media. I have noted how prize winning photographs in salon photographic competition have been less meaningful to me as they relate little to my memory and senses. Those casual shots of street scene and people become more meaningful instead.

Sometimes life is ironical, we begin to treasure the seemingly insignificance only after we have lose them.

It seems, as photographs aged they take on a bigger role and fill in our memory gap, and make us complete by conciliating our existence to our past. So get a wide angle camera and start shooting general scene and let the image aged and take on an age old pastiche.

50. Flaw makes a picture loveable

Do you always think of making perfect pictures? We all do. With that we always come up with reasons to acquire more equipment. We upgrade our gear to more expensive one, each time we use them we are more worry of damaging them than using them. We treat them too well to be used. We tape them up to protect them, scratch proof them, keep them in the dry cabinet. Eventually selling them away because we either felt they were not fully utilised or the value of cost over usage was too high. Then we resign to the fact that we have no time to perfect photography as it needs more of our time and we don't have them. Wow! A bag of excuses, we don't just give excuses for our failures during work but we also give excuses to ourselves during leisure.

What if we forget about making perfect images and just enjoy photographing?

Will that make us more willing to experiment? Would that take the pressure off us to buy more equipment and spend more time on it? And if photography is fun and not perfection, wouldn't it be relaxing when photographing. With this mind set, I believe it takes the notion of cost off our mind. We are not looking for return or evaluating how much it is worth.

There will never be a perfect image. The perfect image is the ideal state, which is always there to beckon us and each time we get nearer, it seems even further away. Each image we shot is a feedback and we use it to better the next shot. Every image has its flaw. We should accept the flaw and move on, as human is not perfect. We should forgive our flaws, we see the same for the image, and we soon learn to love them for their flaws which could turn out to be their uniqueness, a signature of sort.

So with this in mind, any camera becomes a flawless expression of what we see, so continue shooting and enjoy the shots.

51. Creative Blur

I have always believed that photography is about creativity and less about the sophisticated lenses and the cameras we own.

Even blur images have its attractiveness.

If you own a camera that does not take sharp picture, you can be creative and made the most out of blurry images.

Here is a technique to purposefully blur the image to create artistic light-scape. Make long exposure for night scene by adjusting to smaller aperture, so that it is greater than 1 second. Select buildings that are well lighted, compose and than move the camera to create the effect you want. First execute a simple movement of diagonal, horizontal or vertical. Check your image. Analyse the image and see which movement makes it better and nicer, think out of the box, you can do curve movement too. You can attempt something slightly more varied, an 'S' shape movement. I did and I was pleased with abstract images of blurry lights and colours.

Now pick up your camera and hit the night street to create more 'Creatively blur' images! Create your own success story.

52. The treasure is under your nose

Legend always has it that treasure hunters travel far and wide, went through hell and danger, beat difficult circumstances with wits before they could discover the treasure. This myth always stays with us. No matter what, a treasure inherently requires immense effort, be it an outward journey or an inward journey, of vast landscape and geography or of the soul and the mind. A search plus an undaunted effort will eventually lead us to the treasure or treasured.

Is this necessary? Can you phantom treasure without effort? Can you phantom treasure without seeking? Can treasure reveal itself before you?

You take notice, pick it up and therein lies in your hand, is your treasure.

What a nice feeling, effortlessly, peacefully and calmly treasure comes to you. Must you be blessed before you can have it? I always wonder? And I am curious.

All the treasures are appearing and fleeing before us. We need to notice them, frame them and release them. Always wear your camera if you want to pick up the treasure. Be receptive and ignorant, always be ready to receive and it is easier to be given that way. See it as it comes, receive it with gratefulness and respect.

53. Escape from the camera

It is a classic motif in legend and modern drama that the recurring theme of too much love can turn into hatred and hurt. A loving mother or a loving spouse devoting their entire life for their love one without having something for themselves turn haunting when their love is not reciprocated or things did not go the way their love one want them to be. One should always be fearful when you are receiving or giving undivided love. It smells of storm brewing in the distance future. Didn't you ever feel trapped within too much love and care? We all do. We felt contrived and caged. The anguish we experienced could be a sudden outburst of anger or silence endurance. They make great epic tragedy. Perhaps you would say I am a coward; I flee and retreat to safer ground.

I flee from my love, my camera. We were inseparable and I love the camera so much that I was intoxicated. I spent 24 hours shooting, developing, and viewing the photographs. I spent less time on other things. I was oblivious to any opportunity passing by. I was irritable and blared off at the slightest distraction. My attention was camera, camera up grade, better camera, and I saved everything for improving them. I was trapped in the adrenaline rush, the intense concentration, the unceasing thrill in technology precision. The camera is a piece of Art in it self. Needless to say, no matter how much attention I put into the camera and understanding every technical aspect of it, my creation stagnated. I was incapable. I saw great images from Nikon Annuals and was perplexed and awed by the images.

I am a firm believer of intuition. A voice came. It told me to put away my camera and the solution is outside the camera. I did and I have benefited from that decision. The separation was initially unbearable. I felt incomplete. I was going through the 'you complete me syndrome'. However, I experimented and started to develop ways to reduce this incompleteness, to find a new pictorial landscape. Soon I was freed from my camera. My eyes and imagination took great flight, I was freed, and I was achieving free reign.

I realised that creation lies outside the camera, the camera is a tool, and it is a great revelation. Though it was a painful process, the end of it was joy and bliss. One practice I developed during this process is to sit quietly and observe the surrounding, pick something that interests or touches me. I would frame the image in my mind, crop and obliterate the unimportant. I projected my consciousness to another position to frame the same subject, see and feel the differences between this new one and the last one. I projected more positions, moving again, up, down, left, right, in, out and adjusting the depth of field.

Without the camera, I am free and I have taken more pictures than I can imagine. I have experimented more and learned a lot about the subject. I repeated the process many times and guess what? I could have taken million of pictures in mere months. I definitely could not do that when each shot of film was so costly.

One great lesson I learnt and hold dearly, love too much and you are trapped in your own love, learn to loosen it and you will grow.

54. Colour management

If you are very detail and particular on the colour of the photographs you have taken, you would probably find difficulty achieving the colour you prefer. Colour is illusive. It is very difficult to pin down. The same material changes colours at different times of the day. Daylight is warmer, more yellowish, in the early morning and it turns cooler, bluer, later in the day, until it again becomes warmer when the sun is setting. Materials reflect their colours and cast tint on their environment. A blue room will cast a blue tint on the skin of your model. Colours are always changing subtly at every moment due to the changes of the sun angle and the passing cloud that momentarily shields the sun.

Colour shift from camera to camera, display to display and print to print. You should have already noticed that different cameras produce different colours of the same scene. Some may have selected and purchased the camera based on the colour they prefer when they reviewed the images on the tiny LED. The sensor for the same camera deteriorates as we use them and over time, resulting in shift of colours. The camera should be sent for recalibration after some period of use to achieve better colours.

When the photographs are reviewed on the computer, they look slightly different in colours again. It is again different when we compare one LCD screen colour to another make by different manufacturer. Whenever we present the photographs using projector, we would immediately notice the wash out colours. Some colour adjustments have to be made on the projectors, but we will never be able to achieve the same colours as the desktop LCD. Projectors also need a dark room to bring out all the saturated colours of the photographs.

All images displayed by LCD monitor or projectors are temporary and they disappear when we off the electricity, they are meant to be temporary. The light bulb's strength also deteriorate through out the life span of the bulb, which affects the projected images.

The most tedious is printing them out on photographic paper, canvass or other medium. All prints fade, it is a matter of how fast they fade or how sensitive are we to the subtle changes in colour. For printing, the display is only a reference; test print should be done before blowing it up to a large print. Subtle colour adjustment can be made electronically to achieve the print you envision.

I adopted the attitude that colours is illusive and no one is right about which colour is correct, it is an impossibilities, so colours should best portray our intention and thinking instead. It gives me more freedom and possibilities.

55. Blue tone

Not all the time a monochromatic image with Black and White tones is going to portray the emotion you had adequately. Some images' emotional impact increases greatly when it is turned into Sepia colour, some are suited to remain in colour. So how do we decide when we should use which option?

It is about the understanding of colours, colours are considered warm if they are nearer the red spectrum and cold towards the blue spectrum. Consider the feeling and the atmosphere in the photographs or the feeling you want to create and check it with the inherent possibility within the image. I love blue toned images as much as Sepia colours, but it does not suit every subject matters.

The great thing about digital images, unlike in darkroom printing, is that we can improve the image in daylight and there are a myriad of possibilities with image processing software. I can change the colour with simple sliding of the bar or changing some numbers. To achieve blue tones, here is the quickest way I usually do it, open the files in Photoshop, change the mode to Grey scale, then change it to 8 bit RGB mode, open the colour control dialogue box and slide the bar towards blue spectrum, stop only when I have reached the effect I had intended. It is great to look through images and continue to improve the image. With digital post processing images gain huge potential.

I would advise any keen photographer not to disregard the importance of post processing. You have more to gain than lose.

56. Sepia print

You have some very ordinary colour images, you love the smile, hand gesture, facial expression and you wonder how to make them more attractive, give them a new lease of life, regain a sense of the romantic moment. After many experiments, I discovered by turning them into Sepia prints, they become precious memory sought by friends and relatives. In the process, I won accolades too. It feels good and I am motivated to snap more photographs of people. It is a great way to stay connected to friends too. One thing I noticed is that by changing to Sepia, it helps to remove distraction from the background and helps the viewers to focus on the subject. A tighter crop helps to realign the view too.

One application I frequently use is Photoshop. First I convert it into Black and white, then reconvert them back in to RGB mode, then I adjust the intensity of the Sepia colour by manipulating the Blue and the Red sliders of the colour correction command. There are other applications like the iPhoto which has the one button conversion to Sepia colour. It is much easier to accomplish the task.

New Year and Christmas period is a good time to view old photographs, retrospect, give new meaning to past events, and give your old photographs a new Sepia tone wash. Get your old hard disk fired up and start processing. Learning from the past is a way to move forward. Have a great time retrospecting before you make a new resolution.

57. Pastelmatic

Black and white was frequently used during the film days and it never ceased to stir up the romantic feeling in us. Till this digital era, we would still convert colour images into black and white to bring back that nostalgia. Why are we not able to create other tone or colour that is at once representation of this digital age and able to capture the romantic feeling? I had thought about it for some time and my answer to this is what I call 'pastelmatic'.

The image's hue and saturation is reduced to near zero and left with a tinge of perceivable light colours, in pastel nature. By adjusting the CMY (Cyan, Magenta, and Yellow) component of the colours, we can further create different pastel biases. It can be warmer or colder. During printing coloured ink will be added because there is still a tinge of colour. This creates wider perceivable tonal range. You will realise the photograph looks more attractive.

Try it and see for yourself the feeling you can create using this variation.

58. Posterization

If you have seen the work of **Ansel Adam**, you will be amazed at the tonal range of his black and white prints. He had developed a method known as the **zone system** which helped him to achieve the wide range of tones. With digital camera, this can be easily achieved and displayed on the monitor, but the gradation of tones may not print out well on ink jet printer.

On the other extreme is the lack of tones, consider reducing the number of tones to four shade of grey and black, this reduction process of tones is called **Posterization**. During the film days, it was a chemical process to reduce the tone or reduce colour to a few flat colours. However, for digital it is a simple process, using Photoshop, it is one click with an entry of numerical digit. You can change the number as you wish and see the effect changes instantly. It is less popular now, but it was considered a special effect only few knew the darkroom process.

Try Posterization with photograph manipulation application (Photoshop) and see if you could create art, the like of **Andy Warhol** with a click of the button. Of course the selection of the subject matter with iconic stature is the significant of Andy Warhol's art. You may ask why some artists are so famous when their work is so easily achievable. Yes, it is a big mystery of art and great art. I don't have the answer for you but I would advice you to keep searching and experimenting, with a body of work, probably you may have a chance of being great too!

59. The Beauty of Grain and noise

For the puritanical having grainy pictures are a deadly sin and they prefer to invest heavily on their equipment. It almost spells doom for those of us who do not have hundreds of thousand to splurge. **Perhaps sometimes we should see the perfection in the imperfect.** At times we tend to see the tree and forgot the forest. Wouldn't you agree with me the importance of recording the event is having images of the event rather than not producing any image because the camera is not good enough?

Not having the best camera should not stop us from taking photographs that move our souls. In the past, many serious photographers had taken a liking for the graininess of the photographs which they purposefully shoot with high ISO. In the good old days of film, we went as far as pushing the ISO from 1600 to 6400, by 2-stops underexposed and compensate by processing longer to accentuate the graininess. The best camera is not a substitute for creativity.

With digital camera, upping the ISO is as easy as flicking a dial. At high ISO the digital noise sets in and most of us would clinch at the slightest noise. I had always learned to work with the limitation or rather the possibilities of my photographic equipment to accomplish assignments or project. **Addressing the noise issue was for me to accentuate the noise such that the image looks more attractive with the noise and create a new visual landscape.** Creating uniqueness in the image is more important than having a great camera.

Of course, who does not love a piece of great equipment! We always dream of having the next piece of excellent camera, but meanwhile it should not stop us from shooting and creating.

60. Crop away

It was a taboo that portraits of people should not be cropped. It is believed that the head and neck should be intact. Otherwise it garners bad luck. However, some rules are meant to be broken, just for the heck of it. Don't we sometimes love to break the rules and said to ourselves,

"Hack the rules, they are meant to be broken!"

I started to experiment with cropping the hair and forehead of people. The most daring is to slit the head right down at the middle. There was a little eerie feeling when I did it the first time, although it was just an image, but after doing many horizontal and vertical slices, the effect wore off. There was so much tension and discomfort only initially. Later, I saw the benefits of having minimal image that tells a story and the redundancy of having the complete portrait. I begin to see some light in the practise as a way to trim fats from the image and make it lean, mean and concise.

Now, are you feeling the urge to go through all the portraits you had taken and slice through them? If you are, draw them out and start slicing, you will feel the thrill and become more concise in your work. Post them in Flickr or Facebook and solicit opinions from others and see their reactions. Learn from the opinions and improve on your cropping skill.

61. Stitch up when the angle is not wide enough

Have you ever felt that you needed a wide angle lens while doing your routine fun photography? I did. When confronted with the monstrosity of the aeroplane my trusted point and shoot camera wasn't wide enough. A quick solution came to my mind. Just shoot multiple images and stitch it up later. I couldn't miss this opportunity. How often do we get to photograph beside a carrier so huge? I was glad that I had shot those photographs before the airport guard stopped me from photographing. I immediately smiled, waved and apologized before scurrying away so that he had no time to investigate further and delaying my flight. Well, after the 911 incident, people are suspicious of photographer snapping in public areas, decreasing the fun we derive from the camera.

Once awhile good thing pop up from the most unexpected places or events. Here is one genius software that is free and beats other paid software from other vendors – **ICE by Microsoft**.

I had done stitching on other occasions. My wide angle lens was not wide enough to capture the full congregation during an outdoor concert, but no sweat, I shot a few frames and stitched them up into panorama. Everyone is included! I Love the slight curve of the stitched up image.

62. Black and white HDR

It had been a long time since I had used a red filter on the lens to achieved higher contrast for black and white film. One of the unique characteristic is the darken sky, because red filer cuts off blue light, therefore the sky appears darker and more dramatic. It has tremendous attractiveness. On the digital camera, this method was hardly used.

Many of us still love to have the darken sky with pronounce and dramatic cloud.

To achieve it, I use the High Dynamic Range application (HDR). However, as in all HDR at least 2 consecutive photographs have to be shot at different exposures. The application will use the two images and integrate it into a single image by combining the shadow and the highlight area. The resulting image will have more details and clarity. Tripod will have to be used for shooting the photographs to ensure the images stack perfectly.

One draw back is that for moving objects, there may be ghost effect appearing on the resulting image, which are very annoying. However, it is perfect for inanimate objects such as buildings, street furniture, and still life. I use application such as Photoshop HDR function or Photomatix. It is a simple post processing process, try all the sliders in the application and have fun playing them while creating work of art.

63. HDR for Architecture

Architecture needs blue sky to bring out its characteristics.

A saturated blue sky on a sunny day would require patience, not to mention the rainy season when the rain are so unpredictable, it could be a very difficult long wait for sunny day. The best time is the early morning and the late afternoon when the sun is warm.

When photographing architecture, look for interesting shadow that helps to add interest to the photographs. Often, if we expose for the sky, the shadow area and the plants would look dark and lack detail, while the light coloured wall would look washed out.

High Dynamic Range (HDR) photography is necessary to bring out the amazing quality of blue sky and lovely green of the landscape.

Tripod is necessary for mounting the camera to ensure no movement during the multiple exposure, otherwise blur image will occur after combining them into a single image.

HDR cameras are more than 100 thousand dollars. A cheaper way is achieving HDR using post processing application. Of course more work has to be done after shooting the images. For post processing HDR, a few photographs have to be shot with bracketing exposures.

Application such as Photoshop or other specialized software such as Photomatix is used to post process the various images, it combines all the detail in highlight and shadow area resulting in more details and richer colours. It brings architecture photography to another pictorial possibility.

64. Imbue image with meaning

Undeniably, we are motivated or moved by certain event or impulse to snap the image at the particular moment. It is the first instance of instilling and affirming the worthiness of the image. It does not end there because photographs are meant to be read again and imbued with a second deeper reading. It is through this second reading that it would generate more readings and increase the worthiness of the image.

The photographer, in this case, as the creator of the image or the founder of the image must be the first to give it value by mere pondering, musing, appreciating, elaborating, explaining and deepening the meaning of the image that would eventually allow the image to attain its full potential.

Photography does not end when you snap the picture. It is the beginning of its life. Its birth needs a continuation of attaining more meaning and develops its full potential. Similarly, learning does not end when one obtained his or her university degrees.

Learning is a continuous process; we learn as we grow.

The primary responsibility of the photographer is one of revealing and elaborating its meaning and fulfilling its existence. Of course in some cases, after bringing the birth to a certain maturity, the piece is able to grow further through its own meaningful existence, eventually entering into the collective memory of the masses, cutting across culture and geography. Such is the power of the language of photography. It is universal.

A two step approach should be adopted by all photographer, the before and after process complete the process of photography, otherwise it remains as time passing, remaining in the temporality of being without ever been expose to its eternal destiny.

Bring out all the past photographs and start the second reading process. You would relive your experience and learn from them. **Share the photographs and your thoughts with others to be complete.**

65. Know your uniqueness

You would have noticed whenever you passed by a row of apartments, you could discern the unique smell and flavour of each unit. This is also true for photography, if you have scrutinized thousand of photographs by different photographers and compared them, you will find the flavour and uniqueness of each photographer.

I have been taking insects and spiders for 6 years now. My other activity after taking the picture is to crop, scrutinize and appreciate the image. I could see the differences and uniqueness in my photos after carefully comparing them with others.

To understand your work is to see it in the light of others. Initially you may not see it, but continue to browse and enjoy others' work.

Slowly, after a prolong scrutiny, some special unique vision will come and you would be enlightened.

There are 3 stages to the making of the photographs, the shooting, the post processing and lastly the state of mind enjoying the photographs.

Experience them and you will feel more fulfilled.

66. Simplicity: One camera, one lens, one shot

As we grew up, things seem to get increasingly complex. Life too gets more complex. Digital cameras have more buttons and dials. Flashes can have a variety of attachments and we are lost for choices. It takes more time to read the manual before getting down to real fun and before long a new model is launched. We never stop upgrading to stay in the forefront of technology. In all this rush and adrenaline driven excitement, we devoted less time to shooting greater photographs. We are weighed down by the amount of equipment we have to carry. Wouldn't you get tire of lugging so much weight around the shoulder and you wished you could have one perfect lens that does it all? We know one lens does it all would remain forever in our dream, but what is possible is reducing our desire to have everything, carry only a single camera and only one lens, shoot with the perfect shot in mind using a single shot.

Yes, change our attitude towards perfecting the image instead of chasing the equipment, one camera, one lens and one shot.

Be prepared to disregard your urge to bring more lenses or cameras, bring a single lens and get out there, see and shoot. The best place to practise is to roam busy street where activities are abundant, you would be drawn into the picture by the dynamism of the place. Your adrenaline level would rise and you tend to see more opportunities and great moment. The best is to start with a wide angle lens, such as the 35mm or the 24mm. The 35mm f2 for the dSLR is a suitable standard lens for the non-full frame dSLR. With only one lens, you are forced to learn how to move forward or backward to compose your picture and soon you will learn to move left, right, up and down to achieve better result. Have fun feeling the lightness and singular mission. You can have more choices too when you are more engaged with the place and people. You are coerced to see and shoot instead of constantly changing cameras and lenses.

67. Learning to ask

Most of the time, you want to shoot portraits of people and you are too timid to ask. There is always the first time. Look at it this way, the more you ask, the more you are good at asking. I am always chilled when I asked and get rejected, because asking is a request which has either a yes or no answer. If it is no, ask another person until you get a yes. There is a saying, "Ask and you shall receive". Of course, when asking please be specific, and don't be general, otherwise you may be rejected due to vagueness. Few people will oblige when the request is too vague.

Always smile when you ask and ask with confidence that you will be getting an affirmative answer.

The secret to getting people to say yes to your request sometimes has to do with the place. I found more successes at the beach. I usually stroll along the beach, smile and look for happy and jovial people. I shoot a few general scenes and then when they noticed me, I would politely ask them for their portraits. Most of the time, I am very successful at getting their portraits. I would take down their email and sent the images to them. It is important to send them the portraits you had taken. By doing that you would get to build a relationship with them and gather comments from them. It is only fair that they get a small token of appreciation from you, a 3R postcard.

Once when I was in Philippines, doing a study on tourism at Boracay beach, I shot many portraits of tourists whom I had met locally from different parts of Philippines and from as far as the middle east. I asked and all of them obliged to have their portraits taken. I saw and captured so many happy faces. One memorable thing I did was to print the photographs I had taken and scrolled along the beach a second time to give them the photographs. They were very thankful, exhilarated and I was satisfied.

Try it the next time when you are touring. You will definitely not regret doing what I did. Have fun!

68. Shoot Portraits with Macro lens

Have you ever seen the beauty of illuminated skin and wished that you could go near them and photograph them? Or have you been attracted to ageing faces full of history and story? Or that you just love every detail of your lovely new born.

You want to photograph all of them in minute detail.

You can use the macro lens to achieve this. I used the 100mm macro for extreme close-up portraits. I was please with the result. I could capture more details in well lighted outdoor spaces. Morning sun and evening sun is the best in lighting up their faces and bodies.

69. Wide angle portraiture

Seriously, why can't we use wide angle lens to capture portraits?

We can. The pertinent question is why we want to do that and what are the benefits or shortfalls of using wide angle lens for portraiture. One great shortfall comes to my mind immediately is the distortion cause by wide angle lens. With a wide angle we include more of the surrounding; we can get nearer to the subject; we can create more dynamic images and we can obtain more acute angle. If distortion is not very important to the subject then we would have more ways of composing the image, otherwise, we may have to position the subject in the middle where there is least distortion. With wide angle lens we still could get a shallow depth of field by positioning the subject near the lens with the largest aperture. Tilting the camera slightly would add more dynamism to the image. Often the foreground and the sky would seem empty if there is no supporting interest or subject within those barren spaces.

Another great advantage of the wide angle lens is that it can distort and perfect the figure of female models. It has a lengthening effect if the subject's legs or arms are position nearer to the ends of the picture. Model will look slimmer with lengthy legs. Try it.

70. Portrait lenses

For those who began photographing during the film days, it was very popular to immerse in portraiture armed with the 105mm lens. Portraiture lenses were made in the focal length of between 85mm to 105mm, manufacturers labelled some of these lenses as 'portrait lens'. Some have soft focus effect built into them, so that the blemishes on the face are eradicated through the abundant overflow of light. With the introduction of dSLR and sensor smaller than the full frame dSLR, the equivalent of the 35mm film cameras, the question of what is a good portrait lens requires re-evaluation.

After owning a few of the fixed focus lenses and experimenting with them, I couldn't find significance differences between shooting portraits with 50mm, the 100mm or the 150mm. Of course some would exclaim it is the depth of field and the lens speed. I could only pin it down to one most crucial point, the working distance with the subject. The 100mm on the smaller sensor dSLR requires you to be further away from your subject. You have to raise your voice to communicate with the model, which would impede communication.

Intimate communication is required between the photographer and the subject.

Moreover, with the 100mm lens, shutter speeds also need to be increased, hand has to be more firm to hold the lens, the lens is heavier, camera bag needs more space, price of lens is steeper, as compares to the 50 mm.

There seems to be more disadvantages then advantage, but it all boils down to individual taste when it comes to good portraiture, what works magic for others may not work for you. Before you buy any lens for portraiture, look through others work, make detail comparison and check what you can afford, but nothing beats investing in good optics because it brings you clarity and sharpness. They last too.

71. Using 50mm 1.8 for portraiture

For those using the non full frame dSLR such as the Canon 500D or the 50D, the 50mm f1.8 is a suitable lens for shooting portraits. The working distance is closer than the portrait lens such as the 105mm or the 85 mm. In fact, the 50mm 1.8 is a runaway bargain for beginners, the lens is handy and light, on the pocket too. It cost about US a hundred. I had used it and with great sunlight the colours are fantastic. The only fall back is the sluggishness of the auto focusing, a little slow compare to other lenses.

Even when the weather is a little cloudy, with the f1.8 aperture, I am still able to bring out the colours and create nice bokeh. A shallow depth of field is good for isolating and bringing forth the subject.

This 50mm standard lens never failed to impress me.

I learned from those who have used this lens that most of them are pleased with the result. I never stop recommending it for photographer who have budget constraint or prefer to have a lighter lens.

72. Shoot from high angle

There was a time, when I was wondering how I could grow taller and get those precious shots from a high angle. I thought rather than having the conventional shot from my eye level, I could experiment with high angle shots. The ladder came in useful. I had been using the ladder for elaborate model shot from high angle but when I am going about documenting street scene, events were happening too fast and I became so clumsy with the ladder.

I thought for some time and found the alternative use of the monopod and a remote control. It works so much better and it is more efficient.

For now, monopod is a necessity whenever I roam the street with my camera.

I have done many interesting shots and gain a new perspective of seeing the street scene. I began to learn how to position my mind's eye at high angle, anticipate what the camera could see and shot with more precision. It was like out of body experience where I could replicate an alter-self looking down at the same scene while I was physically standing at the ground position. It helps me to see and experience different perspectives.

73. Using Wide angle lens for event

I love to shoot events with a super wide angle lens. I used a 10-22mm lens to cover events such as wedding, baptism and product launch. Some places are cosy and small which require a super wide angle lens to take in the length and breadth of the event.

The beauty of shooting with wide angle lens is that I do not need to worry about focusing problems, as the depth of field is very deep. Even at the aperture of f3.5 at 10 mm, most subjects in the scene will be sharp. However, the only one thing I dislike is that due to the wide field of view, things at the side are distorted. Human beings look elongated as they move to the edges. In most cases, it would include plenty of empty space or uninteresting non-event. The solution is to crop them to a ratio of 2:1, a long panoramic. The cropping helps to focus the subject and convey succinctly the message of the photographs.

Getting near to the subject and clicking at the right moment is important in creating a dramatic image.

Keep that in mind and you would capture those precious moment and eternalise them. Never stop experimenting with super wide angle lens! The more you use it, the more you can get out of it.

74. Low angle shot

During Christmas Season, the huge Christmas Trees are back. Haul up your camera and get down to the town centre! **Shooting from the ground upwards will create spectacular views** and most of all, the whole Christmas tree could be filled within a single frame.

With digital camera, laying it on the ground and shoot upward is an easy process. It is simply, shoot, review and re-shoot until you get the image you want. That way, you need not lie on the floor. Do a test shot and review the shot by replaying it in the camera. Then adjust the next shot until you get the shot you envision. Of course the wider the lens, the nearer you can be with the Christmas tree. There will always be people lining up to get their photographs with the Christmas trees. Being near can avoid being block by people who try to get ahead of you.

There are also special Christmas tree which allows photographs to be taken from inside.

Low angle shots are also useful when shooting track and field events. It put the runner in the same plane as the floor and their facial expression are clearer, especially during the start of the race.

75. You are the zoom

I have always advised many people starting photography to buy a standard lens as their foray into photography. However, the first question they would ask – can it zoom? They have a tremendous affinity and urge to zoom into things or people, especially beautiful people. Yes, the standard lens of 50mm for the 35mm film camera, the 35mm for the dSLR or the 20mm for the 3/4 sensor can zoom into people.

You are the zoom! If you want the subject or people to be big, walk nearer to them before you snap their picture. Some would say, but people will get angry. They prefer to shoot from a distance and reason that it is not possible to go near them without annoying them. Here we realized the phenomena, many photographers prefer to engage others from a distance and stay remote from their subject. The results are pictures that are detached and lack connection. A picture shot from a distance is different from one shot in proximity.

You can try taking one from far and another nearer. Compare them, feel, hear and see the differences in the picture. Keep scrutinizing them. The day you see differences in them, you would have felt and seen something beyond which I can describe here. Use that understanding and you will benefit from it.

There will always be excuses for not trying.

Keeping those excuses and you would still be where you are. Any harm if you try?

I guess **it is a challenge of your humility and your fear of going near the subject!**

Loose the fear factor and you would emerge a better person, a fearless one. Now, isn't it something nice to have?

76. Photograph those who want to be photographed

We always thought stranger would be uncomfortable and in some cases would feel offended if we photographed them. Why is that so? Could it be our timid action which causes this reaction? Their reaction would probably change if you are a well known photographer scouting for images to be included in your next monograph of portraits. Most people would welcome it and are pleased to be chosen for your next book. It is like 5 sec to stardom.

So you got to practise and practise till you are not just good at photography but you are so confidant and unafraid in front of stranger, and you exude the stature of a great photographer, the invincible image hunter. Eventually you will reach a state when it is only your consciousness and your imagery pursuit which remain, not the stranger around you or the fear in you.

How can you start? I started by overcoming the impetus to bring up my camera and aim it at stranger. I would smile and walk up to them, ask them whether they mind me taking more of their pictures. If they prefer I could send them their pictures. They would brighten up and usually it is a positive response. I would write down their mail or email addresses and send them their photographs later. We would struck a cord and started to converse. More people would participate and in one instance in Dubai, I was requested to take more people and their portraits. I was treated as a great guest and they form groups to be photographed. People's reactions from different culture and geography vary. I never know what to expect whenever I went out photographing.

I could only conclude that when you photograph people who appreciate you photographing, it is a better feeling than when people reject your camera and you.

So slowly I grew to move away and stopped photographing those who do not welcome my camera and me. Soon I realized the power of the law of attraction; I became more popular and felt more satisfied with my work.

77. Train yourself to look into the eye

We know good portraits engage the viewers and the **secret is in the eyes.** The photographer has to snap at the instant when the subject's eyes connect with his consciousness. Looking into stranger's eyes is simpler said than done. Most of us avoid direct eye contact when we see stranger, though we might have been introduced. It is a skill to be acquired so that you can look into their eyes without inhibition.

Here is an exercise which you can try with friends to improve your self confidence and interpersonal skills. It could also help you to reduce inhibition when you interact with others.

First you can ask a colleague or friend to sit opposite you with your knees and her knees touching each other. Start with one minute gazing into her eyes without talking. You may feel inhibition initially and have the urge to move the gaze away from the person's eyes. Slowly you may feel more comfortable. Next you can practise by further increasing the timing to 3 minutes, 5 minutes or 10 minutes. Change another friend or colleague to have more practices.

Once you had enough practice, try shooting portraits and check if the exercise have helped you to improve. I am quite sure it would, because I have better portraits after I had removed the inhibition of looking into the subjects' eyes. Both eyes must engage each other to create those eyes that say something.

78. Have no fear

Have you ever been impressed by street life while touring in other countries? And you want to record them, but find that you do not have the courage to go right up and photograph them. Most of us would remember the trepidation. We were worrying about intruding into their routine and we did not snap the photographs which we desperately wanted to record.

It is our fear of strangers, unfamiliar places and getting closer to strangers, that we stood far away, and tried to capture the subject.

We were too far away and the proportion of the subject on the photograph was too small to make an impact.

One way I have overcome this is to take a couple of pictures, hang around for a while, smile if they look at me, and steadily move nearer and nearer, eventually getting better shots. This technique has been very useful. Try it! Stir your courage a notch up and with more practices, you will be pleased with what you are photographing. In time to come, you will be glad you had taken that first step.

79. Selective focusing

Have you ever been in situation where the background is very cluttered and the subject is not standing out clearly? Such situations are not uncommon. In most occasions we would like the subject to be clearly shown to illustrate our ideas and not be distracted by the background. I learned from experience that **one of the ways to make the subject stands out is selective focusing.**

Through selective focusing the focus object will be sharp whereas the foreground and background are rendered blur. The technique is fairly simple, first start by focusing on the subject you are emphasizing, freeze the focus by depressing the shutter release slightly, usually there is a beep sound when it is in focus, shift the camera to compose the shot and then fire the shutter. One important point to note is that the aperture must be set to the widest. You can also increase the background blur by using longer focal length lens or reducing the distance between your subject and your camera.

A wide angle lens, can also have a blur background contrary to the myth that it only has a deep depth of field. By positioning the camera very near the object and using the widest aperture possible, we could still practise selective focusing and emphasized the object. Try it out and see for yourself.

80. The Sun is the heart

After many years into photography, I realize that I have become a worshipper of the Sun. When I started photography, I looked at the weather for decision before I would proceed to the shooting location. I only started to get out of the house when I had predicted that it was going to be a sunny day with deep blue sky. Of course the deep blue is less deep in the Tropics when compared to that of the Mediterranean. The blue sky is always worth the wait.

Photography was an expensive art during the good old days of film, each shot was costly and I had to make sure every shot count. The sun is best and beautiful when it rises and climbs until about 10:00am. We wouldn't shoot again until it is about 4:30pm and continue till sunset. During the wait, there was always the urge to shoot, and I did shoot sometimes, sure enough I regretted my action. No building or scenery looks great on a cloudy day. After 30 years of observing the sky, I have gained enough experience to tell the weather and predict the effect it would have on the photographs. The sun is an omnipresent giver of light, it filters into every corner of our space and lightens them up. Deep blue sky is good for architecture and scenery shots. It helps to give a bright and happy feeling. It provides a complementary background to the buildings too.

For black and white film, I would add a red filters and the sky would have a dramatic effect, as red filter cancel the blue light, less light would strike the film. Till this day, I am still waiting for the right blue sky when taking architecture and scenery. It never goes wrong. One may think that shooting interiors has less to do with the outdoor lighting or the sun. It is very wrong. The diffuse light coming through the windows also lightens up the interiors. During dawn or dusk when the sky is a darker blue, interior shots with huge viewing windows takes on the blue hue and the outside is visible through the windows, creating a well balance colourful interiors with windows looking out towards the warm exteriors.

Waiting for the right sun, tracing her paths and intensity is important in capturing her magic on film. I grew to be so attached to the Sun that I have decided to shoot using existing light for the portraits of the Arthropods. In short, macro-photography, using nothing else excepts the macro lenses and the camera. Again I look out for the sun. It is the giver of form, texture, pattern, and sight. All the magic that I have seen through the lens is painted by the sun. The sun is the heart of photography. Tracing her glorious light and following all her subtleties we can capture her generous offering. **Place the sun in the centre of your heart, see her in her light and shadow.** You will begin to see, sense and hear her through the songs of other animals. The joyous light is the painting of brilliance. Embrace her and rejoice!

81. Shooting against the Sun

When I first started photography, the number one taboo for me was to shoot against the sunlight. It was always better for the sunlight to come from the sides. For portraiture, the morning sun or setting sun was better than an overhead sun which would cast dark shadow on the eyes.

However, as I grew and dwelled deeper into photography, **I realised that I have to re-evaluate and revisit those taboos and prejudices I had acquainted along the way.** For a fulfilling life, we too have to constantly evaluate those life experiences and see how we can live beyond those limitations. Although they had served me well, they also prescribed the limits of my explorations.

I started experimenting in shooting against the sun and I learned a few valuable lessons. There will be flare and contrast deteriorate adversely if the lens is not well designed and made. For those better lenses, it will not have flare. **Over exposure is required to compensate for the area in the shadow. I over expose at least 2-stop.** Glittering light in the background and foreground creates dreamy effect which are captivating. It never fails to draw attention from the viewers. I am addicted to shoot against the sun for many occasions. Once you get the hang of it you wouldn't want to let it go. However, one should try to let it go. One should never stagnate in a particular style. Give it a try!

82. Shadow is light

Raining days are romantic and we love to immerse in its coolness and our laziness. We love to capture the moment, the raining scene, however, no matter how hard we have tried we see a blurry scene but not the rain. In movie, we feel every drop of the rain. We would wonder where did the rain go and what happened? Do you want to know? I was exactly in the same situation and perplexed for a long time. Answers always appear after we searched and spent enough time on them. Light can only be seen when there is darkness. Light is not pronounced in a white or translucent environment. Importantly, light needs to land on material to become visible otherwise light's path is not visible.

In a clear afternoon, within a fresh and non polluted environment, did you ever see the sun rays entering or shinning into a room? I don't remembered seeing it. We always see sun rays filtering through the foliage in the forest during dawn. The sun rays are miraculous. **The rays could be seen because it was made visible by the dew.** Dew droplets are small water particles in the air which are so minute that they fill the space when the temperature is cool and the air is still. If we remove the dew, the rays will disappear. It is the dew particles that the light has struck and reflected which then become visible to our eyes.

Now why we did not see the rain? There are a few reasons, not just one, depending on how you had composed and taken the picture. Rain drops must be situated in front of a darker background, a white streak of water on white background means the rain droplets merge into the background; we would not see them. **The different in lighting must be more than 2 stops or 2 EV.** Otherwise the difference is too little to have an impact. Add filled-in flash to light up the rain, creating a greater exposure difference; it might help. The second reason could be the rain drops are too minute, smaller than one pixel on the sensor, so it becomes too minute to record the rain. To focus on the rain and have bigger droplets, focus on the nearest plane the rain is striking and bouncing off, this enlarges the rain so that it is much bigger than a pixel on the sensor. You also need the correct shutter speed to capture the rain in a streak, too fast they are in frozen transparent droplets, too slow they cannot be seen, so start by using a shutter speed of one-sixtieth of a second and change it faster by a stop for the next until you could see the rain. If you are still not getting the rain, read through this article again and see where you have missed out. Try again and you will succeed in getting the rain in the photographs.

83. Side lighting

I always shoot portraits using existing light and make the best use of the situation. **Windows and doors are the best elements that help to bring diffuse light indoor.** I would position the subject near the windows and make minor adjustments to bring out the character of the subject. The most difficult part of portraiture is not about arranging the subject but capturing the subject in their most natural state, a state where she is her true self. Working with the subjects and building rapport are necessary to make them feel relax and willing to let their guard down and be themselves.

Side lighting emphasizes the profile of the subject and creates a very distinct line of brightness on one side of the profile, thereby bringing out his three dimensionality. The background should be darker to provide the contrast and emphasis for the facial contour and body curvature. I would position the subject next to the window or door, moving them nearer or away from the window to regulate the contrast of the lighting.

Of course the strongest side lighting can be achieved by having the subject directly in full sunlight with the light coming from the side. The sun should not be overhead but at an angle. The preferred time is during dawn or dusk when the light is more subdue and warmer. The same lighting can be used on small animal such as insects and spiders. They would look fabulous when bath in strong side lighting. Give it a try!

84. Shooting landscape

Today, new range of lenses have no depth of field markings on them, maximising depth of field has become more difficult. **Depth of field is visually acceptable sharpness before and after the focused point.** With the old lenses, if we want to have a deep depth of field, we select the aperture and match colour coded depth of field markings beside the focusing ring. We could also use a stop-down button to check depth of field visually. Having the markings is a favourable feature. Without them we couldn't estimate or have a sense of the depth of field for a certain aperture, unless we snapped and reviewed the image. One thing we know is that to achieve huge depth of field we do not focus to infinity, and we should be using the smallest aperture. However, too small an aperture we may have blurry corners. We have to be reminded to use the correct shutter speed to freeze the subject in motion otherwise we may blame the blurriness on the aperture.

For shooting vast landscape we would prefer to have the maximum depth of field. Here is the rule of thumb which works most of the time, focus at one-third distance away from your camera, recompose before snapping. If you need more accuracy, nothing beats shooting one shot and then scrutinising it in detail to determine the setting for the focusing ring. Always use a tripod for detail work, as you would have fewer things to grapple while checking your shots. Remember to set to manual focus before trying this method for landscape photography.

85. Flowing energy

We learned the beauty of stop action photography at high shutter speed but we had not seen much of the beauty using slow shutter speed, except the soft silk like water flowing around the rock or water diving down the waterfall. These are the most common uses for slow shutter speed photography.

Slow shutter speed traces the moving water, visually eliciting the flowing energy, the kinetic energy.

It gives a dreamy effect to movement by blurring the moving, and triggering a romantic feeling in us.

This is how it is done. The lens is set to the smallest aperture such as f22 for most lenses, some older lenses may go right down to f32 and the large format lens can go right down to f64. (There was a club call Group f64, and Ansel Adam was one of the members.) However, even at f22, the shutter speed on a bright day is one-sixtieth of a second. You could use a density filters to reduce the light and slow down the shutter speed further. If the shutter speed can be reduced to a few seconds, it would be great. Of course for such slow shutter speed, a sturdy tripod is required for the process. So that the picture is not just blurry water, there must be some immobile objects such as rock, stone, pebble or trees; they create a contrast between the moving and the stationary elements.

The same technique can be used in many situations especially when there are movement and stationary subjects in the scene, such as trees with swaying undergrowth of grass or buildings with moving cars or crowd. Be creative in using this technique and exploit the wonder of slow shutter speed photography. Capture the flowing energy!

86. Master of time

Modern life in the cosmopolitan is filled with buzz words such as stress, stressed out, too much work, tire, aching, headache, sick, and last of all 'I don't have time'. How marvelous if we are master of our time and not a slave to it? Time. How did the concept of time enter into our consciousness, hold us ransom, and make us its obedient slave. Deadline! Or Dateline! We feel the quiver of fear. How many of us can truly confess that we had tried and could not get out of it.

If you think that the accuracy of measurement of the watch, right down to the hundredth of a second is daunting, get ready for this – a simple point and shoot camera gets you right down to five-hundredth of a second! Is your head splitting now? You are going to explode! The high-end cameras go right down to eight-thousandth of a second. That is really blasting speed. At eight-thousandth of a second, splashing water becomes clear, transparent, instant frenzy ice sculpture that has an instant life span. The camera allows you to control and freeze material in time. Now, feel the freeze and you will get a sense of clarity. If you had already developed the sense of lag in you and your camera, your visual acuity can rise to the next level.

Drawing an analogy from water, we can see that everything around us is in motion and constant flux. Everything moves and becomes stationary on film if a high shutter speed is used. They seem to be still if their rhythm is synchronous with us. Meditation and seeing silence is a way to move in rhythm. The shot is great when the photographer is in rhythm with its subject. A genesis occurs! As we never see the image we snap before it appears, total synchronization and rhythm is necessary to capture the instant that we perceived without perceiving.

Mastering time is an unconscious affair. When you are in it, time becomes your creator.

87. Seize the right moment

With sufficient intelligence and hard work we could learned all the technique of photography, but that does not necessarily make us a good photographer or possess the ability to create exciting work. We need to be discipline, get up early to catch the sunrise or get up earlier to wait for the right moment for the most beautiful sunrise. It is about waiting and knowing when to click the shutter. With detail observation, you could seize the right moment and make it eternal. We do not miss the opportunity; we seize opportunity just in time. This makes a good picture, a good picture.

During the five years that I have been shooting Arthropods, I have only seen the wasps nibbling spiders once. It was a cloudy day, in sheer coincidence, we saw two wasps working in pair, attacking spiders that were perching in the middle of the orb web. Beside me, I saw one falling attaching to a single silk. I tried to help, but he was too badly mangled, a sign of irreversible eminent death. Sensing that the wasp could be back for more, I took one step backwards. As I had guessed, the wasp came back and started to tear the abdomen of the spider away from the Celophathorax. There was no better moment than this moment. I set the ISO higher and quickly fired the shutter away at the wasp while it was too engrossed to notice me. I seized this opportunity and made the moment permanent. I am always ready to get into action. This readiness is crucial in moment like this. Once you strap on the camera, be ready to shoot all the time and never miss any shot.

Seizing the moment is an ever ready attitude which one should adopt.

Adopting it is a step nearer to producing better photographs. Cultivate the attitude and you will benefit from it for life.

88. Photography is discipline

You have seen hectic market places and bustling trading ports. You have seen many photographs of sunrise and sunset. You love the colour and their serenity. You love the great lighting that illuminates and highlights the people, accentuating their face, sweat and activities. You see them in great details and you are awed.

Behind all these great photographs are the immense patience and perseverance of the photographers.

You saw pictures of great moment when the goal keeper leaped up with his arm stretched out and the ball touching his finger tips with the striker in the background exclaiming and wishing that it is a goal. It is an intense moment, a peak motion shot. Did you know how many times the photographer have practised and patiently waited for this moment to arrive? He might have replayed the shots and visualised the precise moment thousands of times. He has to be ready all the time to snap this moment. We only saw his success and share his joy, but not the practices and failures he had gone through.

Like any other sport or martial art, photography needs discipline. You may think that it is plain luck to have shot picture in such wonderful moment, but it is not, it is opportunity that presents itself and you must be ready to take it in the nick of time, at a few thousandth of a second and with precision. It needs many practices with strict discipline to be able to do that. Sometimes planning and rehearsal are needed too.

Here is a practise I did when I was starting out, or when I am handling a new camera. I would pick a subject, focus, click and then pick another then focus again and click. I would change exposure if the lighting condition changes. I would practise until I am satisfied with my speed of focusing, composing and timely release of the shutter. I only need to control the shutter speed, the aperture and the exposure compensation button to achieve the image I envisioned. That is why I prefer less dials and features. I would consider other features redundant.

Be creative, invent practices which you think would help you to improve your photography. Different areas of photography require different skill sets, so be specific when you train yourself in handling the camera. We must treat the camera, as the racket is to badminton or the rifle is to the sniper.

89. Photography is joy

We might have been asked or we could have asked ourselves many times what is love? Some would say give and take, or give and receive. Others would declare triumphantly love is unconditional and when our love is not reciprocated, we sank into a low state affirming love is scarifies. We felt like great heroes and martyrs. How do you think a martyr would feel at the moment of his death? Do you think the feeling of death is joyous and light? Have you ever been in the situation that your love is unrequited? Yes, I am referring to unrequited love. Have you?

Love is a feeling, a joyous feeling, a state of the heart for some and others prefer to call it a state of the mind.

Do we feel that we are sacrificing when we are enjoying? No! We felt something fleeing and valueless, a feeling most often money cannot buy. I always experience unrequited love. My lover is Layla, photography.

Photography is about joy, not about scarifies, or having an objective or wining or giving. There is no other in photography. It is only photography. I have adopted this loving attitude towards photography and I am still loving it. Everyday when I am photographing, it is bliss! You can adopt this loving attitude too and feel the joy. Wouldn't you? If only you are feeling the same for your lover, everything will be simpler, but why not, it is that simple after all.

90. Not getting it is a feedback

Have you ever asked yourself why you love photography so much? Should there be a reason for loving someone or something? Perhaps we do not need a reason. Even if you have a reason. Does it helps to improve and better your photography? Probably not. If a mad man put a gun on my head and ask me the same question, 'Why do you love photography', as I am now imagining, my answer would be that **there is no failure in Photography**. As photographer we shoot, read, scrutinize, crop and look for the next great image. There is never an end or a beginning, just shoot, shoot more, enjoy the photographs, and shoot some more. It is a continuum process of eternal lure and infinite possibilities. There are the chance meeting, the purposeful and the meaningless, all dissolving into a single creation with a click, which cannot be recreated. Thrilling!

Do you feel lost or down whenever you miss a shot or not getting good images as you would have expected? You should not, photography is a process where you look at your photograph and learn from it. Every picture is unique and cannot be recreated except printing it from the same digital file. Inherently this is a plus point. There is something good about it even it looks bad for you. Every picture good or bad is a feedback and nourishment of our spirit. So adopt an attitude that every photograph is a feedback and enjoy the thrill of shooting.

Remember, every good or bad photograph is a feedback. Go get the next one! Photography is a continuous process.

91. Curiosity is not enough

A technically superb photographer or photographer wannabe will point you towards the fact that you need a great camera to shoot great picture. To a certain extent, I would agree with them that you need good camera to shoot a technically clear and crisp picture. However, to be a good and great photographer, it is not necessary to have expensive and great camera. Some great pictures can be taken with a reasonable point and shoot too. So what makes a good photographer? Curiosity is one of the ingredients to being a good photography wouldn't it? Not really, you may say, because a kid is curious and he is not a great photographer. I can understand the comparison and that is why curiosity is not enough. With curiosity, we investigate and clarify our queries. We learned from it, we translate the learning into implementation and experimentation. We refine the experiment by developing more curious queries until we are more refine in our approach.

Always be curious and look for subtle differences, because any substitute is not the original copy.

Let me reiterate, be curious, clarify and learn, implement and experiment, query the result and refine it.

When I was starting out, I was curious about the effect of different apertures on the photograph. After repeated checking with senior photographers, the answer I got was that when the day is sunny use f16, in the shade use f5.6 and in darker area, use as wide an aperture as you can, but the picture will not be sharp and it depends on how good your lens is.

I wasn't satisfied. I went to the library, checked the books and magazines on photography. I learned from my unceasing quest that aperture is one of the most important factors in creating good photographs. Images look different when different apertures is used in the same lighting condition. The decision on which aperture to use is less dependent on lighting but what is the intention of the photograph. It was a great revelation.

Till these days, I am still curious about many things and everyday I am learning. My photography improves too. It is important never to stop learning and experimenting. **Get curious, find out and implement. It goes a long way.**

92. A distilling process

I always suspect that we would eventually fall in love with a place, however conventional it may seems to us initially, if we constantly visit the place and get acquainted with her, for that matter, most of us love our country, though some of us nag about her inadequacy because we desire more. However, deep down our roots had already gone deeper. Our country has an unspeakable association with us or we have an unspoken love for her. It is the *genius loci* which *Christian Norberg-Schulz*, spoke about. The relationship is built up through a long drawn process of distillation till it becomes part of us. How can you acquire a sense of a place? By a quick visit to the place, like a hurried tourist? As it is the photographs you had taken in these places would only reveal superficial understanding of the place and your hectic character.

The Spirit of the place can only be felt by repeated visits at different time of the day, and with an open attitude to absorb all things bad or good about her.

Only with the commitment to spend time and the willingness to understand her, then we are able to distil the her essence and experience the thrill, the prolong fermentation, would age like old wine. I would make countless visits to the same place to work on her. For some places I continue to visit them over a period of 30 years. I see them changed, matured, flourished, deteriorated, and rejuvenated. I captured and registered them. I could see the differences and uniqueness all within the same picture and outside the picture. They become more meaningful and they have a story to tell.

A place needs to be distilled like the process of producing wine.

93. Persistence

Perhaps we are afraid of things we do not know much about, once we see them often, larger and clearer, they may become adorable.

I learn a lot from nature and the micro world of insects and spiders. They constantly inspire me and I have continuously benefited from them. Nature is such a powerful source of energy which often renewed our vigour and empowered us to do more things. With nature, we found more energy and passion; we are alive and rocking.

Nature is all around us, from spiders and harvestmen to ants and wasps. I could still remembered after being inspired by the colour and form of crab spider which I saw in Inner Mongolia, I decided to photograph insects and spiders back in Singapore but I could not find many of them. They were so well hidden. I pondered a lot about where to find them and each time I was disappointed. All I could find were common dragonflies, damselflies, ants and butterflies, I wanted to see more varieties of form and colour. I never accepted it as failure, as each try I had, I received a feedback, and I would try again. Then I did the simplest and the most tedious method. I chose a bush, formed a mental map of a gridded space of about a metre high and two metres wide. I would diligently scanned from left to right then down the next row and left to right again. I went through each leaf and branch. My persistence paid off, I found an ant mimic spider feasting on a young grasshopper. It took me almost fifteen minutes and diligent scanning to locate this interesting Arachnid. I was grateful to have found this little fellow and my curiosity garnered more understanding from the entomologists in the *World Wide Web*, from whom I gain knowledge and utmost understanding of these arthropods.

Persistence and patience is the path towards good photography. Acquire persistence and you will gain greater satisfaction from photography.

94. The descent

Lying prone on the grass floor is not so difficult to execute when compared to descending on war zone or the most filthy place that you would imagine. There were many occasions that you felt it was beneath you to get to a degrading position to photograph them. You rather stay far away and shoot with your long telephoto lens. You wouldn't want to be near or be involved intimately. You want to live on the other side, observing from a vantage point, making comments and remarks about them, you always think you know their live.

Seriously, it is difficult to empathise from afar without getting involved and getting near. As a tourist we will always feel disgusted with the amount of filth and poor people when we visit over populated and under provided places. They were always rushing towards us and they were eager to make a little more from us. Sometimes they had to cheat a little to get a bit more. We would be flabbergasted, extolling the virtue of honesty, as if we are blessed with godly virtue. Sure, as a photographer, a diarist of life, you want to bring out the struggle in their life and the difficulty they have to face. You want to show their plight to the world. You also want to bring a piece of them home as souvenir. We are proud to show them off to our friends: photographs of their face, hands, and clothes. They are such a beauty and we feel great about our photography.

We make beauty of them devoid of their context and struggle. Would you want to be a tourist photographer or one who portray reality accurately? If the later is what you aspire to do, then descend from your vantage point, learn to be humble, spend time and effort to get to know their stories. Be prepared to spent weeks or months with them. Perhaps then you could bring out their live story and portray them accurately. You would eventually understand their live and empathise with their behaviour. Your work would reflect your humility and your understanding of their circumstances. You would bring something good out of them and would not think that you are going to be a great photographer because of the time you had spent. You would hate to think otherwise.

Only by descending to the lowest depth, we will finally understand the greatness of humility and be a better photographer.

One should not take life so seriously that you bring their grief with you and drown yourself in their sorrow, or kill yourself for your helplessness. One should adopt a gratitude that nature is such. Human beings are just an insignificant part of nature. We are not all powerful and above all other beings, we do the best we can. We are mortal. Continue to shoot photographs and be a better person. It helps to bring out the goodness in human nature.

95. Sleight of space

Do you want to be able to shoot pictures where people in the scene are not aware of your presence and even they do, they allow you to photograph them willingly? If you can do that, your images would look more natural. It is as if you are invisible. Do you realise every one of us has a personal space that extends beyond our physical self? If a stranger comes too close to us, we will feel uncomfortable or irritated. Of course, with your love one, this space would reduce tremendously. It also varies according to culture or country. This space has a smaller radius in country such as China and India. Perhaps due to the sheer size of their population and their adaptation to congested spaces. Their behaviour would alarm foreigners, who would feel that their personal space are being invaded and constricted. This may arouse the foreigners' hostility towards the locals. Be mindful so that you do not get beyond someone's personal space when you are photographing, otherwise you would see their discomfort within the picture.

Another space is a shared space within a certain community or a group of people. For example when you walk into a street lined with *café* and art galleries, some store holders or frequent visitors could feel your presence. Some would notice your actions and movements even though they may not be looking in your direction. If you photograph immediately, they would be alarmed and become uneasy with you and your camera. However, if you allow yourself to choose a humble place and settle in, try sitting or standing at inconspicuous corner, slowly their attention would turn away. While you take time to postulate those images you want to take, you become part of the scene and the space. Of course it is good to smile and node your head if you see them looking your way. **Everyone loves a great smile, so practise your smile until it is great.** Persistently, you have marked out your presence and territory. Fiddle with your camera and very confidently bring it up to your eye and start photographing. By now, most people would not know that you are photographing and if they know, they wouldn't be alarmed at your action. You had just sleight into the space.

It has work for me. The longer you stay in that space, the more firm is your territory and you would be accepted and allowed more free reign to perform your photographic ritual. This needs some practices, and more practices will get you nearer to the subject. Remember to acknowledge their presence initially and then leaving them behind is important for you to focus on your subject. Have fun practising the sleight!

96. Enter and leave yourself behind

Are you very conscious of yourself if you stand up among the crowd and walk right up to the subject you want to photograph and snap away? Most seasoned photographers could do that without second thoughts. You would think that they have courage and you do not have what it takes. So you give your intention a pass and blame yourself later for not acting out your intuition resulting in bad images.

You should follow your instinct, focus on the subject. **It is not about courage but enters into the subject and leaves yourself behind.** When you see the subject, concentrate and focus on the image you want to snap, forget about yourself, loose yourself, loose your ego and be nothing. Your own existence disappears. All you could see is the subject. Make beauty of the subject. Remember when you are behind the camera, the camera dissolve you. You disappear. Your consciousness follows the subject and steals those moments. You are one with the subject.

I practise this when I am photographing people, insects or spiders. I am always asked, 'How did I come so close to the insect and why the insect did not fly away?' Then I realized what I did was losing myself. Each time when I lift up my camera, I focus and put all attention on the insect. I see the view changes to the preferred composition, my body, limbs and hand would automatically move in minute distance to allow that possibility. As I move unconsciously nearer and nearer the insect, I get the image I want. Somehow most insects are aware but prefer to ignore my advances. All this time, my eye would not leave the insect. I finally get what I want. So start losing yourself and focus on the subject. I am sure you will improve tremendously.

97. I am the Servant

I am neither religious nor spiritual in nature. I am a free thinker, but I was inspired by a speech delivered during a baptism ceremony. I couldn't believe my ears when I heard, "Jesus is your Servant". Initially I thought I had heard it wrongly. The pastor continued to elaborate how Jesus was a servant and why we should receive his unconditional grace. As a servant, Jesus washed his disciple's feet. Now, there is a contradiction here, the Lord is a servant to his servants. I pondered over it and realized that greatness is in serving others.

Weren't Gandhi and Mother Teresa serving others? And now the latest buzz, the Servant CEO, all that is saying had been said in the great books, one of them is the Bible. How can this servant attitude be relevant to photography, you would ask? Being a servant in its purest form is an attitude. A servant obeys and serves without any discomfort or insecurity. He or she is there to satisfy your needs.

He is oblivious of himself, he focus on fulfilling the needs of others.

Photography, unlike painting, record reality as it is reality. Photography is a servant to reality. Only by humbling and serving, can one bring out the being of reality. We are the silence servants, observing and recording. We do not dictate nor should we arranged them to suit our visual design, we serve. We serve the subject, we serve nature and we serve all. In this humbling attitude we bring out the being of reality, its greatness and its flaw.

Adopt the servant attitude and see the world's magic unravel before you!

98. Dead and awaken

This may be one of the best or the wildest tip I am giving out. We have often heard of people who had near-deaths and *out-of-body* experience. When they came back, they experienced life with more clarity and lucidity. They appreciate the nuances of different flowers' fragrance, see everything in brighter details, take things calmly, become more helpful and see possibilities in adversity. It interests me that they can see and appreciate things with a higher level of acuity. They see clearer and sharper.

Photography is about seeing and appreciating.

With sharper visual acuity, it would bring about betterment of photographing. You have to see what you are taking. Many years back I had a near-death experience. I was in the army training. I over exerted and ended up in a condition known as heat exhaustion. It was the most desperate life threatening situation I had ever been in. My system failed one by one and finally I had no other consciousness except thinking or I think I am thinking.

It all began when I realized I was not sweating and I was feeling hot, I tasted no saliva. I knew this is the symptom of heat exhaustion. First I saw blinking spots of light, they filled up fast, became all white, then bright glaring green and finally black. I lost my sight! Simultaneously I felt ticking effect over my arms and legs, I quickly sat down, there was more numbness, I lied down to prevent collapsing on the floor, my limbs started to vibrate uncontrollably and soon I did not sense my limbs, body, and then in total darkness my sense of breathing was gone. Panic set in, I cursed and cursed, the curse was no avail, then I told myself to cool down, though I cannot sense my breath it did not mean that I was not breathing, so I focused on breathing. I survived, by mere concentrating on breathing. The next day when I woke up, I felt acute pain on every inch of my flesh. I never look at the world the same way again! My fascination for the world has increased tremendously.

Near death has awakened a part of me. I felt so different. It wasn't the actual death, but the mere experience of death which opens a new way of seeing. It is the psychological effect of death, the reason that changes the way we see. Now, do you want to experience a new way of seeing? So if you can bring yourself to a psychological death you could possibly change the way you see things, because we are facing death squarely we will be in tune and treasure things we already have. Do you really want to do this? If you do read on, otherwise skip to the next tips, because you are not ready. Do this with a friend beside you and tell him or her the steps you are taking. Both of you can take turn to do this. Try this at your own risk. It is dangerous. Everything about death is a taboo and a danger, don't do it. Avoid it. WARNING! Adverse effect may happen, do it at your own risk!

Find a quiet place in the garden. Close you eyes, sense your breath, and calm down. Now start imagining that you were seeing beautiful images and having the happiest moment of your life. Continue the happy memories for a while. Now imagine that the picture is filling fast with blinking stars, they fill up fast and you are seeing brilliant white light then suddenly it is all darkness. You are alone. Now you start loosing your limbs one by one, you loose your body, you loose your lungs, you loose your neck, you are residing in one part of the head, and the head is slice bit by bit until your consciousness is left in a speck of dust and no bigger. You see this speck floating, flying, you see light, you see nothing, you vanish! VANISHED!!! You see what you could see. When you have enough, reassemble the head, the neck, the body, the limbs and you are full again. You are back and alive.

Open your eyes and you would see the world differently. You see and you photograph. Enjoy your life!

99. Keep a journal

As we already know, heard or read that a book reveals as much about the story and about the author. The author lay exposed at the second layer of the text, his understanding, his opinion, his thought, in essence as the conjurer of the text, we see too the conjurer, his cleverness and prejudices, his fear and courage, his intelligence and short coming, his beliefs and superstitions.

All is said, in the photograph, we too could see the photographer's genius and his foolishness, his patience and anxiety, his thought and omission. Forgetfulness is one of essence and weakness for the photographer, we see, hear and learn a lot from the places we visit, we assimilate those experiences, grow with them and become restricted by them. It means a lot to us, as human beings we sometimes need to be reminded of our thought and revelation. We need a journal to record them, otherwise, brilliance is not retained and served as a reminder, point of clarification or springboard for the next creation.

I always keep a journal with me because whenever I am inspired I can quickly make notes of the idea.

The journal is the mental code that helps us to organise and clarify our thoughts.

A journal can be sketches, bit and pieces of text, incongruent thinking, queries, problems' notes, solution, arrows and signs. We can use colour to exert marks and signs on them. A journal is a gibberish mental map which only the owner can decipher those literary marks. It provides all the ingredients and substance for all our fun. I sincerely advice you to keep a journal close by to help you in your photographic journey. It helps to track your development as a photographer too.

100. Forgetting and contradiction

We learn as we mature in our craft. We assimilated the lessons we had learned, made them into rules. Slowly they become part of our habit that we never again question their relevance or grew to be unaware of their existence, until, may be, someone younger or bolder begin to question them, insisting on some answers. We would think for a while and provide them some answer, which sometimes they may find the answers not relevant, however they do mean a lot to us and we would stubbornly held on to those rules. These rules have worked for us and made us what we are. They had liberated us, enlightened us, are the reasons we are successful and respected. We also have to realize that they too are our prejudices and fears.

Time changes, things change, cameras change, preferences and taste also shifted. Perhaps we should not hold so tightly to our beliefs or habits. Perhaps we should move with time and revalidate our rules for their relevance, be a little more energetic and forward looking as when we were younger and bolder.

Perhaps, sometimes we shall be forgetful and contradict ourselves, as in a state of amnesia. In so doing, we may see new meaning.

So you too shall look inward conscientiously at the things we are holding dearly and see if there are more ways to creating master pieces. Have fun!

Acknowledgement

I would like to thank the following for their help and encouragement.

Cheryl M. Cordeiro-Nilsson
Poh Fatt
Catharine Cook
Dr. Mel Gill
Yee Poh Chun
Gigi Wang
Eric Kwa
Steve Lee
Regu
Sashi
Eric Tan
Pang Teck Seng
Ng Shuh Fang
Zhu Shengbuwei
Zhu Shengyiyu

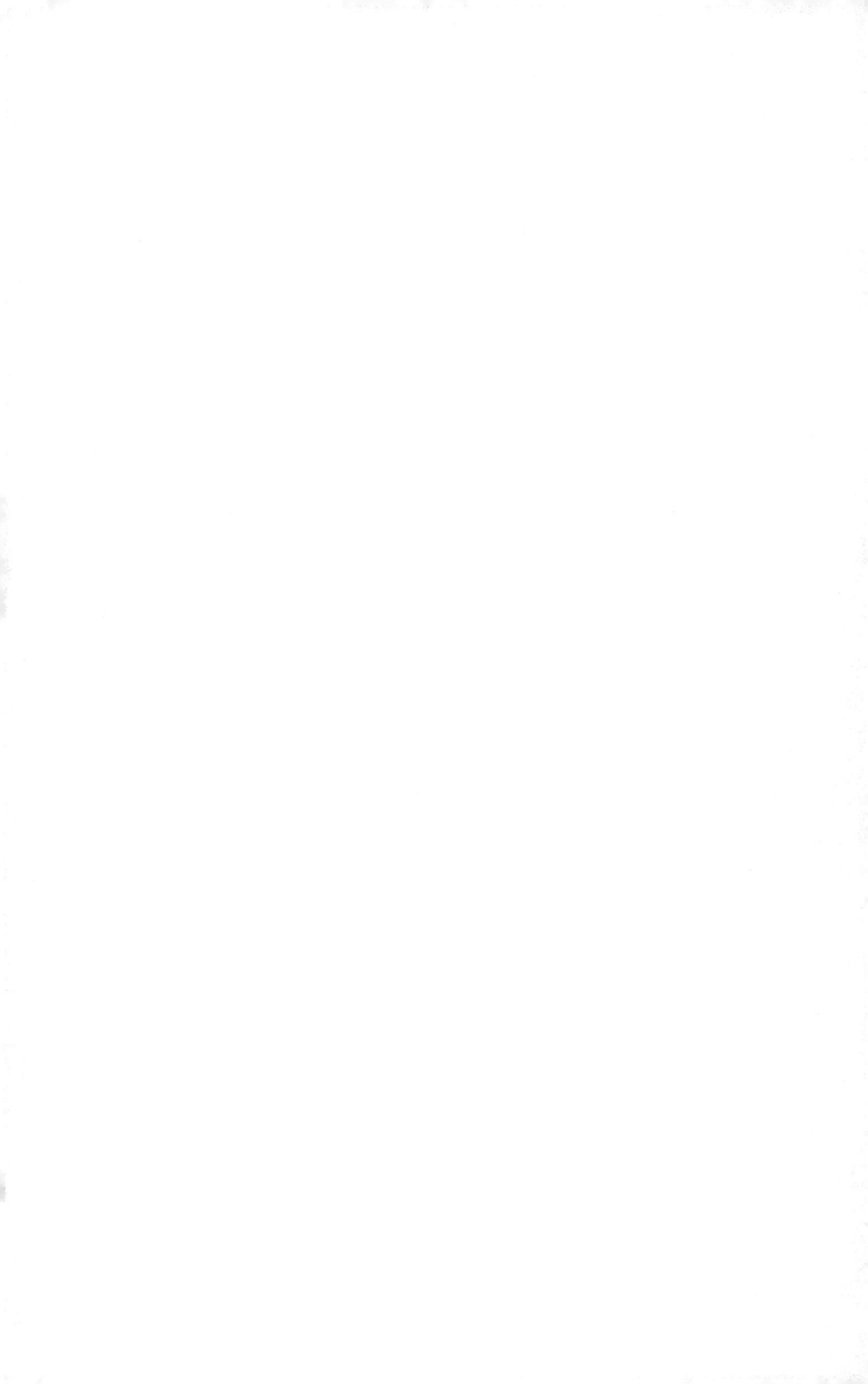

www.ingramcontent.com/pod-product-compliance
Lightning Source LLC
Chambersburg PA
CBHW031422210526
45464CB00005B/2008